SUSSEX
Newton

PASSAIC

BERGEN
Paterson
Hackensack

WARREN
MORRIS
Belvidere
Morristown

ESSEX
HUDSON
Newark
Jersey City

UNION
Elizabeth

HUNTERDON
SOMERSET
Somerville
New Brunswick
Flemington

MIDDLESEX

MERCER
TRENTON

MONMOUTH
Freehold

Mt Holly

Toms River

Camden

BURLINGTON
OCEAN

Woodbury
CAMDEN

GLOUCESTER

SALEM
Salem

ATLANTIC

Bridgeton
Mays Landing

CUMBERLAND

CAPE MAY
Cape May CH

The New

Enchantment of America

NEW JERSEY

By Allan Carpenter

CHILDRENS PRESS, CHICAGO

ACKNOWLEDGMENTS

For assistance in the preparation of the revised edition, the author thanks:

BENJAMIN WOLINSKY, New Jersey Office of Tourism and Promotion; MARY ALICE QUIGLEY, head of Educational Services, State Library, New Jersey Department of Education; and TERRY KARSCHNER, Historian-Curator, New Jersey Department of Environmental Protection, Division of Parks and Forestry.

American Airlines—Anne Vitaliano, Director of Public Relations; *Capitol Historical Society,* Washington, D. C.; *Newberry Library,* Chicago, Dr. Lawrence Towner, Director; *Northwestern University Library*, Evanston, Illinois; *United Airlines*—John P. Grember, Manager of Special Promotions; Joseph P. Hopkins, Manager, News Bureau.

UNITED STATES GOVERNMENT AGENCIES: *Department of Agriculture*—Robert Hailstock, Jr., Photography Division, Office of Communication; Donald C. Schuhart, Information Division, Soil Conservation Service. *Army*—Doran Topolosky, Public Affairs Office, Chief of Engineers, Corps of Engineers. *Department of Interior*—Louis Churchville, Director of Communications; EROS Space Program—Phillis Wiepking, Community Affairs; Charles Withington, Geologist; Mrs. Ruth Herbert, Information Specialist; Bureau of Reclamation; National Park Service—Fred Bell and the individual sites; Fish and Wildlife Service— Bob Hines, Public Affairs Office. *Library of Congress*—Dr. Alan Fern, Director of the Department of Research; Sara Wallace, Director of Publications; Dr. Walter W. Ristow, Chief, Geography and Map Division; Herbert Sandborn, Exhibits Officer. *National Archives*—Dr. James B. Rhoads, Archivist of the United States; Albert Meisel, Assistant Archivist for Educational Programs; David Eggenberger, Publications Director; Bill Leary, Still Picture Reference; James Moore, Audio-Visual Archives. *United States Postal Service*—Herb Harris, Stamps Division.

For assistance in the preparation of the first edition, the author thanks:

Consultant Laurence B. Johnson, Secretary-Treasurer, Educational Press Association of America; Marvin C. Creamer, Associate Professor of Social Studies, Glassboro State College; and Herta Prager, Head Bureau of Law and Legislative Reference, State Library.

Illustrations on the preceding pages:
Cover photograph: Asbury Park, New Jersey Office of Tourism and Promotion
Page 1: Commemorative stamps of historic interest
Pages 2-3: Asbury Park, New Jersey Office of Tourism and Promotion
Page 3: (Map) USDI Geological Survey
Pages 4-5: Sandy Hook area, EROS Space Photo, USDI Geological Survey, Eros Data Center

Project Editor, Revised Edition:
   Joan Downing
Assistant Editor, Revised Edition:
   Mary Reidy

Library of Congress Cataloging in Publication Data

Carpenter, John Allan, 1917-
   New Jersey.

   (His The new enchantment of America)
   Includes index.
   SUMMARY: A history of the state and a view of its industries and sites of interest today.

   1. New Jersey—Juvenile literature.
[1. New Jersey] I. Title. II. Series.
F134.3.C3 1978 974.9 78-14891
ISBN 0-516-04130-4

Contents

America's most famous painting shows Washington Crossing the Delaware *by Emanuel Leutze.*

A True Story to Set the Scene

"D DAY" FOR THE AMERICAN REVOLUTION

The sleet bit into their frozen faces, carried by a wind that had become a gale. As Christmas day, 1776, faded into gloomy dusk, they crouched shivering on the dark river bank waiting for the signal. It was certainly the most unusual Christmas any of them ever had spent.

Ahead of them was an adventure that would demand all the skill and strength and courage they could muster. No one then could have known—could even have hoped—that their actions that night would change the course of the world and prove to be one of the great moments in American history.

As they waited, freezing in the blizzard, the men wondered if the signal would be given at all. Would the whole thing be called off? How could 2,400 men cross a raging, ice-choked river in a howling storm, assemble, and wait on the opposite shore without fire or warmth, march for 9 miles (14 kilometers), and then fight a battle? This incredible plan of General George Washington's seemed an impossible one.

The Revolutionary War had only begun, but already Washington and his soldiers had been pushed all the way across New Jersey by the advancing British troops and their hired Hessian soldiers. Only by a miracle of his genius had Washington been able to gather up all the boats on the Delaware River around Trenton and cross over to the Pennsylvania side.

The British were stopped until they could construct new boats or find others. Also, it was Christmas; they could afford to pause at Trenton to celebrate the holiday.

Clearly this revolt of American colonists would soon draw to a close. The Americans were disorganized, fleeing, lacking in morale. The mother country would have them back in the fold. New York City had been taken by the British. New Jersey was overrun; Washington's troops were leaving his service by the hundreds. A few more defeats and it would all be over.

There were reports that America's Commander-in-Chief, General Washington, was dejected and undecided. Nothing could have been further from the truth.

The general knew that he would have to improve the new nation's morale with some dramatic move in order to keep the Revolution from collapsing. One of Washington's men wrote later that he had never seen the general so determined. Washington made the daring decision to go back across the Delaware and surprise the Hessian troops at Trenton, choosing Christmas night as the one time the enemy would least expect an attack. Even his own men thought such a plan foolhardy. But Washington persisted and, with his generals, laid detailed plans with extreme care.

It was tremendously important that the enemy know nothing of these plans. Though the enemy commander at Trenton may have been informed on Christmas Eve about the proposed attack, the weather became so bad he may have thought it would be impossible for an army to cross the Delaware.

Nevertheless, Washington gave the signal, in the dusk at six o'clock, December 25th, and the first wave of huddled men took their places on the 60-foot (18-meter) long "Durham boats." Gale winds buffeted the boats; great ice floes bore down on them; sleet blanketed them. In spite of every obstacle, the first boats made it safely across.

The first wave of men had to crouch on the New Jersey shore of the Delaware for six hours, without fires, while the boats went back to pick up their comrades, then their horses, and finally eighteen pieces of artillery. The entire crossing took nine hours. The last boats did not reach McConkey's ferry on the Jersey side until three o'clock in the morning.

One of the men later said that on the tempestuous way across the river General Washington talked of farm crops and prices and other everyday matters. He did not stand in the boat nor strike the pose shown in the famous picture. He constantly retained "a serene and unembarrassed countenance."

After all were across, they made good time on the 9-mile (14-kilometer) march to Trenton, in spite of the storm. General Washington's great gamble paid off. The Hessians were surprised and soundly defeated. One thousand fifteen of the enemy were either killed or taken prisoner. Only two Americans were killed in battle, and two died of exposure in that awful, long, bitter night. "Officers and men behaved with great firmness, poise, advance and bravery," Washington wrote later.

Almost as remarkable was the fact that the Americans were able to make the long march back and re-cross the river that same afternoon, bringing almost nine hundred prisoners with them, after having been up all night in the hardships of the river crossing and the march and the battle.

That fight at Trenton was not a major battle in the usual sense, but it might be considered the turning point of the Revolutionary War. News of Washington's unexpected success spread quickly across the former Colonies. Nothing could have encouraged the Americans more. The courage and the will to keep up the struggle seemed to flow back to them with the almost miraculous success at Trenton.

A leading Briton admitted, "Our hopes were blasted by that unhappy affair at Trenton."

So it was that, early in the war in a sort of Revolutionary "D Day," New Jersey played the key roll, as it was to do so often later as the war wearied on.

Lay of the Land

A vast area of marsh spreads over lowlands near the sea, where the tides come in. Here sedge grasses grow 7 feet (2 meters) tall, and trappers lay their snares for muskrat and other small animals. These "Jersey Meadows" have changed little in hundreds, perhaps thousands, of years.

This would not be strange in a remote and unpopulated land, but the Jersey Meadows lie in the heart of one of the greatest population concentrations in the world, within sight of the great skyscrapers of New York City and of New Jersey.

Here is virgin land, viewed by millions of people every week yet almost untouched in three hundred years.

The reason why the Meadows spread an open wilderness in the midst of the busiest metropolitan area is simple. Reclamation of the almost 50 square miles (129 square kilometers) of land has seemed too difficult and costly because of the unstable base. Now developments are constantly taking place, but much of the Meadows still remains.

The Jersey Meadows are only one of the many unusual features that set the state apart.

The broad flat pathway of New Jersey between Philadelphia and New York City has been called the greatest corridor in the world. Those who see only this level sweep of the state would be surprised at the many forests, would marvel that there are mountains and spacious seashores in the state.

Present-day New Jersey has been formed by great forces working over periods of millions of years. At times the land areas have extended out into what is now the sea; at other times, the sea has crept over most of the land. Mountains have thrust themselves up only to be greatly eroded over the years.

About a million years ago huge layers of ice formed in Canada and slowly pushed southward until they covered much of northern New

Opposite: Ducks are found along the marshy shores of the Atlantic Ocean.

Jersey. Four times the masses of ice crunched their way over about the same areas. When they finally melted, around ten thousand years ago, they left great boulders, valleys carved out by the ice, and basins scooped out by the force of the frozen water, now filled with lakes.

Since that time the land of New Jersey has been much as it is today.

Only a few miles lie between the ocean and the highest point in New Jersey, High Point in the northern Kittatinny Mountains, 1,803 feet (550 meters) above sea level.

In far southern New Jersey, Cape May dips a toe into the sea. Whirling waters of the ocean on one side and the Delaware River on the other have combined forces to build up Cape May over the centuries.

The ocean and rivers have a great effect on the whole of New Jersey. Ninety percent of the state's boundaries are water, with the Hudson River on the northeast, the ocean for 127 miles (204 kilometers) on the east and the Delaware River on the west. Only the small, straight 50-mile (80-kilometer) boundary between New Jersey and New York runs across the land. Navigable waters wash 65 percent of New Jersey's boundaries.

In fighting its way to the sea, the mighty Delaware River has cut a great opening called the Delaware Water Gap through the Kittatinny Mountains.

More than a hundred other rivers drain the state, but New Jersey rivers are not of great size. In order of size, some of these are the Raritan, Passaic, Mullica, Pompton, Maurice, Great Egg Harbor, Millstone, Wallkill, Hackensack, and Toms. These rivers are fed by an annual rainfall which makes New Jersey one of the "wettest" states in the continental United States.

There are about eight hundred lakes and ponds in New Jersey, none of them extremely large, most formed by the action of glaciers. Lake Hopatcong is the largest, and others are Greenwood (shared with New York), Mohawk, Budd, Culvers, and Swartswood. The principal lake region of the state is in the north central area.

Lake Hopatcong was formed in the 1750s when a dam was built on

Lenni Lenape Indians Trade with Henry Hudson's Men, *a mosaic made by students of Shrewsbury Borough School for the state tercentenary.*

Brooklyn Pond. As the waters rose, Brooklyn and Woodport ponds joined together to form a bigger lake. A larger dam built in 1831 expanded the lake to its present size, about 7 miles (11 kilometers) long with a winding shoreline over 35 miles (56 kilometers) long.

New Jersey's geography contains a number of surprises.

The Mason-Dixon line is usually considered to separate the North from the South in the United States. If this line ran through New Jersey, more than a third of the state would fall south of it. Cape May is as far south as Washington, D.C. On the other hand, the northern tip of the state extends farther north than New Haven in the New England state of Connecticut.

The four principal physical regions of New Jersey are the Coastal Plain, Piedmont, Appalachian Valley, and Highlands. The edge of the Coastal Plain has served as the great transportation route across the state.

15

*The only mountainous area in New Jersey
is in the northwest, called the
Appalachian Ridge and Valley Region.*

Footsteps on the Land

THE "ORIGINAL PEOPLE"

There is no evidence that New Jersey has been occupied by human beings for more than the relatively short period of 6,000 years. The first known people lived through hunting. Another early group was called the Archaic people. They lived in the area through about 1000 B. C. After that time the early peoples came to be more and more like the Indians who were found in New Jersey by the first Europeans.

These Indians called themselves Lenni Lenape, and the term is said to mean "original people." There were about 5,000 of these original people living in the New Jersey area when the first Europeans found them. The settlers began to call them Delawares, after the river which had been given that name.

The Lenni Lenape were a division of the larger Algonquin Indian group. They had learned agriculture and cultivated such crops as squash, beans, and corn. They had discovered enough of the "science" of agriculture to know that wood ash and fish could be used for fertilizer.

They found game and wild fruits and berries abundant. They had great fondness for sea food, and huge piles of oyster and clam shells discarded by the Indians may still be seen today.

Lenni Lenapes were skilled in making dugout canoes, sometimes more than 40 feet (12 meters) in length. These canoes were hollowed out by burning and chopping away the charred parts with stones.

They lived together in villages and some larger towns, a few of which were crude forts protected by wooden barricades. The Lenni Lenapes called their country Scheyichbi. Until about 1700, most of the contact between Indians and Europeans in the Scheyichbi country was carried on with the traders. In their dealings with Europeans, the Lenni Lenapes were almost always gentle and helpful.

Of course, the Indians used wampum in their trading. Because of the long shoreline and the abundance of shells, New Jersey early became a principal source of wampum. William Campbell actually set up a "mint" in Bergen County near Hackensack to make wampum.

To the Campbell mint came great wagon loads of clam shells from the seashore. Each time another load arrived, all the neighbors were given a free picnic and clam bake. They were asked only not to break the shells, which the Campbells polished and ground into wampum.

Even the settlers used wampum for money. When a ferry was set up from Manhattan Island to the Jersey side, the fare was 6 stivers of wampum.

For years the making of wampum was the biggest business in the area. As fur traders went into the far West, Campbell wampum went with them to buy rich pelts. The Campbells became wealthy not only in wampum but in American money, and the wampum mint was not closed until 1889, after it had been in operation for more than a century.

For the Indians of New Jersey, however, neither wampum nor anything else spelled riches or happiness. As more and more Europeans kept coming in, the Indians were persuaded to sell their lands and move west. No land in the state was actually seized from the original owners.

However, the amounts paid to the Indians for their land were pitifully low, and in most cases the Indians were not aware that they had given up all rights to their lands forever. When they found this out it was too late.

By 1758 only about a hundred Lenni Lenape families were living in New Jersey, and an unusual step was taken to care for them. The colonial government established a reservation for the Indians—the first in the United States. The government bought 3,258 acres (1,318 hectares) in Burlington County, built homes, meeting house, stores, school, mills, and blacksmith shop to help make the Indians self-supporting. A missionary was placed in charge. Governor Frances Bernard gave the reservation the name Brotherton, because it was hoped that all could live together in brotherhood.

But the reservation failed in New Jersey, through lack of government support, poverty, disease, and firewater (liquor), and most of the "original people" left the state for good. Fewer than eighty-five of these unfortunate people were left when they sold their reservation lands for a nest egg and went to live with the Stockbridge Indians in New York. Later they moved to Wisconsin and finally to Oklahoma.

Only one Lenni Lenape Indian remained in New Jersey—"Indian Ann" Roberts. Many of her ninety-one living descendants still live in the Trenton area. In 1958 about half of them came back to the Brotherton region, now called Indian Mills, for the unveiling of a tablet placed to honor the 200th anniversary of the Brotherton reservation.

In 1963 Governor Richard Hughes met with the chief of the Lenni Lenapes, Arthur L. Thomas, and invited the Delaware group to leave their present homes in Oklahoma to visit New Jersey in celebration of the Tercentennial in 1964. And so the original people of New Jersey came back to their first home, if only for a short visit.

Today about the only mementoes of those early inhabitants are the names they left behind: Hackensack, Hoboken, Metuchen, Rahway, Musconetcong, Hopatcong, Kittatinny, and also such common terms as canoe, hickory, sassafras, tobacco, wigwam, chipmunk, persimmon, and papoose.

SMORGASBORD AND WOODEN SHOES

As early as 1497, the white sails of their small ship silently brought John Cabot and his crew within sight of the shores of present-day New Jersey, but the explorer did not land there. Giovanni Verrazano, sailing under French orders, also passed by the Jersey shore, in 1524.

Although there may have been Viking discoverers much earlier, history records that Henry Hudson, sailing under the Dutch flag, discoverer of the river that bears his name, was the first European to set foot on New Jersey territory.

Tragedy came to the Hudson party in New Jersey when a group of his men were attacked by the Indians. John Coleman, shot through the neck by an arrow, died and was buried on Coleman's Point, which is now known as Sandy Hook. He was the first European to be buried in New Jersey.

Who can imagine the thoughts of these early adventurers as the tiny sailing vessel passed into Sandy Hook Bay, then went on to give them the first look at the mighty palisades? One of Hudson's officers, Robert Juet, wrote about New Jersey, "This is a very good Land to fall with, and a pleasant land to see."

The Dutch were not slow to take advantage of Hudson's discoveries. By 1618 there was a Dutch trading post at Bergen.

In 1623 Cornelius Mey sailed up the Delaware River and was able to establish small Fort Nassau on the east shore of the river near where Gloucester is today. He gave his name to Cape May. In the 1630s scattered Dutch settlers made their homes along the Jersey shore of the Hudson.

In 1638 Dutch control of the New Jersey area was threatened by the Swedes and Finns. With Finnish help, Sweden set up a colony called New Sweden along the shores of the lower Delaware River.

To help this struggling colony, they sent, in 1643, one of the most unusual men in colonial history as their governor in the New World. This was Johan Printz. As someone has said, he "looms large" in the history of the Colonies. He was actually so large that the gangplank almost collapsed under his 400-pound (181-kilogram) weight as he walked ashore to take control. The New World had never seen anything like this 7-foot (2-meter) giant. In spite of his fierce ways and stern control, he failed to impress the Indians, who called him "Big Tub."

Printz built Fort Elfsborg and another fort near present-day Gibbstown, but the Swedes neglected their colonies. They never numbered more than ninety-eight people, and after seventeen years of Swedish control, the Dutch took over in 1657.

FROM DUTCH CHOCOLATE TO BRITISH TEA

Early Dutch settlers along the Hudson had mistreated the Indians, and as a consequence there had been Indian uprisings. In 1660, to protect themselves, the Dutch settlers built a stockade and established the first town in New Jersey. Called Bergen, this settlement is now a part of Jersey City, the oldest permanent community in the state.

Dutch rule was not to last long. Remembering the voyages of Cabot and others, the English claimed the land. Holland did not dare dispute the power of England. The English king, Charles II, granted the Dutch colonies to the Duke of York, and the Dutch surrendered their authority in 1664.

The Duke of York parceled out what is now New Jersey to two of his favorites, Lord Berkeley and Sir George Carteret, and called it New Jersey in honor of Carteret's service on the Isle of Jersey.

Elizabeth, founded in 1664, was the first settlement made under English control in New Jersey and the second permanent settlement in the state. Several other settlements came into being within a few months, including Newark in 1666. These settlers were mostly from New England.

The titled owners of New Jersey had difficult times pleasing their settlers. Violence and arguments often erupted over taxes and other matters.

New Jersey was divided into East Jersey, with Perth Amboy as capital, and West Jersey, with its capital at Burlington. This resulted in little more satisfaction for the scattered early settlers. Again, in 1700, the settlers rebelled. Finally their lordships, Berkeley and Carteret, gave up their governing authority in New Jersey. So New

Lord Berkeley and Sir George Carteret *from the Shrewsbury School mosaics.*

Jersey became a Royal Colony in 1702, and the governor of New York took over civil government.

The people of New Jersey resented this leadership of New York in their affairs. A "border war" broke out between New York and New Jersey in 1719 and was not settled for fifty years, when the two finally agreed just where the boundary should be.

Domination of New York over New Jersey was broken in 1738 when Lewis Morris was appointed the first governor of New Jersey. He had little success in dealing with the unhappiness of his people; rioting and dissension continued. The population, meanwhile, was growing. By 1745 it had passed the sixty thousand mark.

Morris' successor as royal governor, Jonathan Belcher, was more successful. When William Franklin (son of Benjamin Franklin) took over as New Jersey's governor in 1763 the colony was calm, but discontent soon began to grow again. The people resented acts of the government and considered it harsh and unreasonable. They felt they should have more control over their affairs and some voice in what was to be taxed, as well as what the rates were to be.

In July, 1774, seventy-two delegates held a convention at New Brunswick to appoint five representatives from New Jersey to the Continental Congress at Philadelphia. Meanwhile, the people were peacefully resisting the acts of the government.

The Boston Tea Party is familiar to all. A similar incident in New Jersey history, a year later has not become so well known. The British tax on tea was hated throughout the colonies. When a shipment of tea was landed in Greenwich, a group of men from Cumberland County put on Indian disguise and "brewed" the tea in a giant bonfire. The date was December 22, 1774.

WASHINGTON WAS AWAKE HERE

After two more years of growing discontent, the American colonies were ready to declare their independence from Britain. The Provincial Congress of New Jersey was in control of the colony and Governor Franklin had been arrested.

22

This was one of the many sad divisions of the Revolution. Benjamin Franklin, of course, had been one of the strongest leaders in the move to throw off British rule. His son, Governor William Franklin of New Jersey, persisted in his loyalty to the English king. This proved to be one of the great disappointments of the senior Franklin's life.

The same kind of heartbreak occurred throughout New Jersey; families and friends were divided as some remained loyal (Tories) and others supported the overthrow of British rule.

However, the New Jersey Provincial Congress made the historic break, and created a new constitution for the colony, making it independent. The first governor of this new independent New Jersey was William Livingston.

Warfare came to New Jersey in November, 1776. In the war years that followed New Jersey suffered four major battles and ninety minor engagements of the Revolution.

New Jersey has become known as the "Pathway of the Revolution," or "Cockpit of the Revolution." General George Washington and his troops crossed and recrossed it four times. It has been called one of the most strategic and most fought over of the thirteen Colonies in the Revolution. General Washington spent more of his time in New Jersey as commander of the armies than in any other area. He was quartered in New Jersey for a fourth of his service as

Washington's headquarters during the end of the eighteenth century, located in Morris County.

Revolutionary leader. It may be said that "Washington slept there." But it would be more accurate to say that he spent some of his most brilliant waking moments there, also.

When General Washington was first forced to retreat across New Jersey in late 1776, the area was thrown into confusion. Many troops deserted. The state legislature dissolved. The British and their hired German troops overran the countryside, looting as they went.

Then came the first Battle of Trenton. Just a week later another battle of Trenton was fought. Then at Princeton a fierce battle saw Nassau Hall changing hands three times. The new nation mourned the death of General Hugh Mercer in this battle, and the county where he fell is named in his honor.

Unfortunately, the long war was only beginning.

Washington and his troops went on to Morristown where they spent the first of their winters in New Jersey.

More than a year passed before the armies met in another great battle in New Jersey. This was the Battle of Monmouth, fought on the searingly hot Sunday of June 28, 1778. Here the actions of strange General Charles Lee might have lost the war. Earlier in the war General Lee had been captured in his nightgown at the Widow White's in Basking Ridge, after refusing to bring his troops to assist Washington in the first retreat across New Jersey. But Washington did not remove General Lee from his command because of this when Lee came back in an exchange of prisoners.

At the Battle of Monmouth, General Lee failed to follow orders for an attack and ordered a retreat instead. Baron Von Steuben was able to rally the American forces, and with the help of Lafayette the battle amounted to a draw—when without Lee's failure it might have been a great American victory.

Some felt that Lee was guilty of treason, but others considered him only incapable. A court-martial found him guilty of leaving the field of battle. His sentence was a year's suspension without pay.

If the actions of General Charles Lee at Monmouth have shamed Americans, the heroism of another American at the battle has thrilled them, even if some of the details are not verified. As the terrible 105-degree Fahrenheit (40.6-degree Celsius) heat of the day bore down on the soldiers, one of the wives, Mrs. Mary Hays Ludwig, followed her husband to the battle and carried water to the soldiers in her pitcher. Molly Ludwig has been called "Molly Pitcher" ever since. When her husband fell in battle, Molly Pitcher is supposed to have taken her place at his cannon and "blazed her way into immortality."

Washington spent the winter of 1778-79 at the Wallace House in Somerville. This was a comparatively relaxed period, with a good deal of social life. At one of these affairs, General Washington proved his admiration for Mrs. Wallace by dancing with her for three hours.

Another year dragged by, and this time the troops went into winter quarters at Jockey Hollow near Morristown. Washington, accompanied by his wife, Martha, set up his headquarters at the nearby home of the young widow Theodosia Ford. To the misfortune of the troops, this proved to be the most awful winter in a century. Although it is not so well known, the winter at Morristown is often considered to have caused greater hardship to the troops than the better known one at Valley Forge, Pennsylvania.

To keep his men occupied, Washington had them build a fort. Since the fort really had no military use, it was given the name Fort Nonsense.

Not even "busy work" could keep the minds of the men from their hardships. Twenty-eight snowstorms swept in, most carried by strong bitter winds. In the blizzard of early January, many men were buried in their collapsed tents under 4-foot (1.2-meter) drifts.

Desperately concerned for the welfare of his men, General Washington wrote, "For a fortnight past the troops, both officers and men, have been almost perishing from want. . . . At one time the soldiers ate every kind of horse food but hay."

The winter was so bad that even in the Ford mansion Washington and his staff and Mrs. Ford and her four children spent most of January huddled about the fireplace in her kitchen. Washington wrote again, "Eighteen of my family and all of Mrs. Ford's are crowded together in her kitchen, and scarce one of them able to speak for the colds they have."

WASHINGTON AND LEE AT MONMOUTH.

AY72.35

A stern General Washington meets Lee at Monmouth.

At a court-martial in Dickerson Tavern at Morristown, a young American officer named Benedict Arnold was convicted of associating with Tories. General Washington refused to punish him except for a reprimand, but Arnold's feelings were hurt, and he deserted to the British within a short time.

A happier note was brought to Morristown at this time by Alexander Hamilton, who found a charming young lady, Betsey Schuyler, living near the Ford mansion. They spent much time together, and she later became his wife.

Spring brought further good news; that great French friend of America, the Marquis de Lafayette, arrived at Morristown to announce that French troops were on their way to help the Americans.

When General Washington and his staff left the Ford mansion in June, he asked Mrs. Ford if all her property was accounted for. She replied that only one silver spoon was missing. Not many days later, a messenger arrived bearing a silver spoon with the initials "G.W." engraved on it. As soon as he was able, the general had replaced the missing spoon with one of his own.

As the war drew to a triumphant close for the Americans, the scenes of revolution shifted from New Jersey, but the region continued to do its part. The Garden State had supplied its bounty to feed the revolutionary armies. Provisions from Salem County helped to keep Washington's troops from starving at Valley Forge.

New Jersey also had been one of the leading iron making colonies. Because they wanted to sell the colonies their own iron goods, the British tried to stop this manufacturing before the war. It was fortunate that they were not successful, because the iron works of New Jersey proved invaluable in supplying for American armies the basic materials for muskets, cannons, and other goods of war.

More than 17,000 New Jersey men fought in the Revolution.

New Jersey played a key part in the postwar development of the country, although this is not so well known outside the state. In 1783 Princeton served as the temporary capital of the new country, and a New Jersey man, Elias Boudinot of Elizabeth, was selected as president of the newly elected Continental Congress.

Painter Emanuel Leutze shows Washington
rallying his forces at the battle of Monmouth.

In a way, President Boudinot may be thought of as the first President of our country. At Nassau Hall in Princeton General George Washington received the formal thanks of his country for his services in the Revolutionary War, and word was received there of the signing of the Treaty of Paris ending the war.

Then in 1784 the capital of the new country was moved to Trenton.

When it became clear that the Articles of Confederation needed to be changed, many plans were proposed. As a small state, New Jersey feared that if members of Congress were selected only on the basis of a state's population, the smaller states would be completely overwhelmed. New Jersey delegates presented what was called the "New Jersey Plan" to the Constitutional Convention. This plan provided for a Senate in which all the states would be equal, with only two Senators each. When this plan was adopted, New Jersey could truly be called "the Mother of the United States Senate."

When the new Constitution creating a United States of America was sent to the states, New Jersey was quick to follow the lead of Delaware and Pennsylvania, and so became officially the third state, December 18, 1787.

Yesterday and Today

New Jersey was hopeful that Trenton would be selected as the new permanent national capital. The city was located in almost the exact center of the new country, and most of the northern and central states thought it would be ideal. However, the southern states would never agree to a northern capital, and so at last the U.S. capital came to stand on the banks of the Potomac rather than on the banks of the Delaware.

In 1790 Trenton was selected as the state capital, instead. For the next several decades New Jersey's population grew slowly.

The effects of the War of 1812 were rather lightly felt in the state.

As more people came to the state, New Jersey pioneered in the building of railroads and canals, and industry began to take a prominent place. Hoboken became a fashionable resort for prominent New Yorkers such as John Jacob Astor, Martin Van Buren, and Washington Irving. In 1844, New Jersey had adopted a liberal new constitution, guaranteeing many of the rights of the people.

The first true game of professional baseball was played on the Elysian Field of Hoboken in 1846.

FOR HUMAN FREEDOM

The legislature of New Jersey passed a law in 1846 to free all slaves in the state, but since the slaves were still made to serve their former masters as apprentices, they were not helped very much.

As the argument over slavery grew throughout the country, New Jersey took a more and more active part. Many New Jersey people strongly sided with the South. The southern states were good customers of New Jersey and many of the people in the southern portion of the state had more in common with the South than with the North.

On the other side, New Jersey abolitionists, who wanted to do away with slavery, played a particularly prominent part in the "underground railroad." This was a network of locations where slaves could be cared for and helped northward from "station" to "station" toward eventual freedom in Canada.

The state remained sharply divided on the slavery question, but when war actually came, there was a great outpouring of Union volunteers from New Jersey. There is a legend that there never was a Civil War draft in the state.

In May, 1861, the New Jersey Brigade was the first to reach Washington, to defend it from Confederate attack. New Jersey's own General Philip Kearny said, "Give me Jerseymen, they never flinch." General Kearny has been called "the most brilliant New Jerseyan in Civil War uniform." He might have been given command of the Army of the Potomac if he had not been killed in battle at Chantilly, Virginia, in 1862.

One of the strangest stories of the war was that of a New Jersey man, Captain Henry W. Sawyer, of Cape May. Captain Sawyer had been wounded and captured and was being held as a prisoner of war in Libby Prison when the southern leaders decided to execute two northern captains in revenge for two southern captains who had been killed by the North.

The names of those who were to die were selected by a lottery and Captain Sawyer's name was one of the two chosen. His execution date was set for July 16, 1863. He wrote to his wife asking her to visit him before his death. She got the letter only three days before the fatal date. Mrs. Sawyer immediately hurried to Washington where she was able to see President Lincoln on the 14th. Lincoln sprang into action with Secretary of War Stanton.

It happened that Union forces were holding prisoner one of the most famous names of the South, General William Henry F. Lee, son of Robert E. Lee. Word quickly reached the South that if Captain Sawyer and the other hostage were executed, contrary to the laws of the war, General William Lee might expect the same fate.

When July 16 came, Sawyer waited for death, which did not come. For a whole month he waited, expecting death each day, but finally the executions were called off, and Captain Sawyer was exchanged for General Lee. They shook hands as they met and wished each other well.

Libby Prison, where Captain Sawyer was held, painted by David Blythe.

Confederate prisoners were kept at Fort Delaware, Pennsylvania, near Salem. The hardships of war prevented the prisoner camp from being properly staffed with medical men and nurses, and the overcrowding was terrible. After the battle of Gettysburg more than 12,000 prisoners were crushed into an area designed for no more than 2,000.

A Federal inspector wrote about this prison ". . . a thousand ill, 20 deaths a day from dysentery; the living have more life on them than in them . . . Thus a Christian nation treats the captives of the sword. . . ."

Thousands of the southern soldiers died. Two thousand four hundred thirty-six of these brave men in grey are buried at Finn's Point National Cemetery.

Those boys from the North who were wounded in battle had no

31

better treatment, simply because there were too many of them and too few to help. One of the most famous of all those who helped the wounded and dying was New Jersey's Cornelia Hancock. She had been rejected for nurse's duties as being too young, small, and frail.

In spite of this, at the age of twenty-three, the Quaker girl took a train for Gettysburg and went straight to the church where the wounded had been brought. There, she was the first woman to take up duties as a nurse. The need was so great no one could refuse her.

Without any real training as a nurse she proceeded to do all she could, making the men comfortable and writing notes for those who would be dead in the morning. She got food for the wounded, whether she was authorized to do so or not. She comforted men whose limbs were being amputated and did everything she could to help.

"The deadly nauseating atmosphere," she wrote, "robbed the battlefield of its glory, the survivors of their victory and the wounded of what little chance of life was left to them."

Later, Cornelia Hancock was invited by the President's office to attend the dedication of the Gettysburg Battlefield, when President Lincoln delivered his famous Gettysburg Address.

Soldiers who had been in hospitals at Gettysburg spent their own funds to have a medal made for her. The military band composed the "Hancock Gallop" in her honor and played it for a review of troops.

When she returned to carry on her work in other battlefields, the secretary of war gave her a pass "to visit anywhere in the lines of the Union Army." After the Battle of the Wilderness she was the first northern woman to enter Fredericksburg, and the first woman of the Union side to go into Richmond when it fell.

By the close of the Civil War, over 88,000 men from New Jersey had joined the armed services.

FROM FOOTBALL TO POLITICS

The need for relief from the tensions of war swept the country and many new forms of recreation came into being. New Jersey took a firm place in the hearts of sports lovers everywhere when the very first official intercollegiate football game was played in 1869 at New Brunswick between Princeton and Rutgers. The lighter Rutgers team won by a score of 6 to 4. Rutgers had to wait sixty-nine years before winning another game from Princeton.

Somewhat earlier, in 1864, the first derby ever run in America took place at Passaic.

The first intercollegiate football game.

One of the unusual events in New Jersey history occurred when in September, 1881, the state was asked to build a railroad overnight to assist the dying President James Garfield. The president had been shot; he lingered mortally wounded for more than a month, but it was felt that the Washington climate was harmful to him. Doctors felt if they could get him to the sea air of the Francklyn cottage at Elberon, New Jersey, he might be helped.

There was no way to get the president from the railroad station at Elberon to the cottage. When the people of the region heard this, they promised to build a spur railroad to the cottage and have it finished the next day. Thousands of volunteers worked all night in the light of locomotive headlights, and when the village woke next morning, a new railroad ran for almost a mile (1.6 kilometers) through what had been an orchard the night before.

The track was too light for a heavy locomotive, so a small one was put on to push the president's three-car train up the spur. The little engine failed to make a grade, and a magazine describes the scene: "In an instant 200 workers put their shoulders to the president's car, the engine's throttle was pulled open, and with a will, slowly and steadily the train was pushed over the grade. Not a shout nor a cheer was heard; there was no noise." The great man was not disturbed.

For a short time, the president felt better at Elberon, but then grew worse and died at the Francklyn cottage only about two weeks after he arrived there. Slowly and sadly the train crew once again drove the train over the spur, this time bearing the president's body on his last journey home.

During the period after the Civil War and on into the twentieth century the most important events in New Jersey history were occurring in the tremendously growing industry of the state.

Along with the growth in industry came a growth of power for those who were gaining great wealth. Railroad and utility interests and other powerful trusts and groups often corrupted public officials and did everything in their power to advance their own interests.

By 1880 the population of New Jersey had reached one million, and many of the people felt that their interests were being trampled by big business and bad government. The trade union movement grew, and several politicians joined the effort to clean up business and politics in the state. A number of young Republican reformers were able to bring at least a part of what they called their "New Idea" into the state's politics. One of the leaders of these was Mark M. Fagan, an undertaker, who became mayor of Jersey City. Three Republican governors, Foster M. Voorhess, Franklin Murphy, and John Franklin, between 1896 and 1910 did much to keep the "Progressive" movement alive in New Jersey, although they are not normally given much credit for this.

The most famous of New Jersey's reform governors, of course, is Woodrow Wilson.

HOLLYWOOD ON THE HUDSON

After Thomas Edison developed the motion picture in New Jersey, that development had an unusual and not generally known effect on the state. The demand for motion pictures was growing in the early 1900s, but few facilities were available for making them.

Early moviemakers began to look for good locations to make their films. One movie group needed a high cliff because their heroine had to be in constant danger of falling off a cliff or faced with some other disaster. The lofty crest of the Palisades at Fort Lee, just south of the site of George Washington Bridge, seemed an ideal spot, and so they brought their cameras and started filming.

The movie serial made there became the *Perils of Pauline,* starring Pearl White. Her perils made Pearl White famous as the greatest star of the serial movies. She always was rescued just in time to keep from falling off the Palisades.

Fort Lee grew as a motion picture center. Between 1907 and 1916 it reigned as motion picture capital of the world. The greatest of the early stars, Mary Pickford, got her start at Fort Lee in her first picture, *The Violin Maker of Cremona.* John Bunny, Marie Dressler, Theda Bara, Mabel Normand, Charlie Chaplin, Rudolph Valentino, and Lon Chaney all made pictures at Fort Lee and added to its worldwide fame.

Important films continued to be made at Fort Lee until 1923, but the title of film capital had long since shifted west to Hollywood.

FROM WAR TO WAR

The make-believe of motion pictures gave way to the harsh realities of war in 1914, with Europe in conflict and the United States was getting ever more involved.

The grave and fearful decision to take America into World War I fell to the lot of New Jersey's adopted son, Woodrow Wilson, and the state quickly was involved with the war in many other ways.

New Jersey became the greatest producer of artillery shells in the world during the war, with 75 percent of all the nation's shell loading capacity. The state led the nation in wartime shipbuilding.

More troops left Hoboken during the war than went out from any other port, and Hoboken was usually considered the major embarkation point of the war.

Not all of the suffering during the war came to the boys overseas. Shortages of sugar, coal, and meat were followed by the awful epidemic of influenza, which killed 17,000 New Jersey people and affected at least 300,000 to a lesser extent.

Strangely, it may be said that World War I actually ended in New Jersey. President Warren G. Harding was spending the weekend at Somerville when the papers ending the war between Germany and the United States were brought to him there. He signed them on July 2, 1921, putting an official finish to that terrible conflict.

MODERN AS TOMORROW

New Jersey gave great encouragement to the lighthearted feeling of the 1920s by starting one of the most famous promotions of all time. The Miss America Beauty Contest was first begun at Atlantic City in 1921. This was the beginning of the great rage for beauty contests which has swept all over the world.

36

"Here she is—Miss America."

Also in 1921, New Jersey and New York created a joint organization to manage the tremendous transportation business which the two states have in the greater New York City area. This was the Port of New York Authority. The authority quickly began to build bridges, dig tunnels, create airports, operate terminals, and carry on all the other activities that make it one of the biggest government operations of any kind.

The Great Depression, beginning in 1929, swept New Jersey quickly, with perhaps greater suffering and misfortune than in many other states because of the many industries of the state.

In spite of depression days, in 1931 the mighty lower Hudson was spanned by a bridge for the first time when the great George Washington Bridge was opened to traffic. It has been said that the opening of this bridge made Bergen County "the bedroom of New York." The bridge is still one of the landmarks of the area.

On the heels of the depression the worst tornadoes in New Jersey history, in 1933, caused over a million dollars damage in Camden and Burlington counties, at Gloucester and Monmouth. Fortunately, no deaths were recorded.

In that same year, another tragedy occurred that had particular meaning for the people of New Jersey. Lakehurst had long been the principal center for dirigibles in the United States. On April 3, the world's largest dirigible, *Akron,* left Lakehurst for a routine flight and never returned. It had broken up in a storm off the New Jersey coast. Only three men, including the captain, were rescued.

Although New Jersey's shores have been the scene of shipwrecks over the centuries, one of the most dramatic and highly publicized took place when the *Morro Castle* burned, with a loss of 125 lives. The black and ruined hull drifted to shore, where it rested near Asbury Park. It proved to be a great free attraction.

One of the most spectacular accidents in the history of transportation occurred at Lakehurst in 1937 when the huge German dirigible *Hindenburg* came in for what was expected to be a routine landing after a trans-Atlantic flight. Highly inflammable hydrogen was used in the zeppelin, because the Germans had no non-burning helium.

While hundreds on the ground watched, the great ship exploded in a vast sea of flames while still in the air over the mooring mast. Radio announcers who had been covering the landing gasped out the horrifying details to listeners all over the country in one of the few firsthand live reports of a major disaster.

Passengers leaped to the ground from the flaming ship with their clothes afire. When the great burning gas bag settled to earth, other passengers could be seen fleeing across the ground, silhouetted against the searing flames. Thirty-six persons died in this tragedy, which brought the era of zeppelin transportation to an end and marked the decline of Lakehurst as one of the most important aviation centers of the country.

Far more of New Jersey's people were involved in World War II than in any previous war in history. More than 560,000 New Jersey men and women served in the armed forces, while almost all who remained civilians took some part in the war effort. The vast manufacturing ability of the state was turned toward producing war materials. During the period 1940-45, Curtiss-Wright at Paterson built 139,000 airplane engines, the greatest output of any single maker. New Jersey shipbuilders turned out an amazing number of the largest warships, including battleships, aircraft carriers, and cruisers.

One of New Jersey's most unusual contributions to the war effort was to furnish fine boards of the finest grade oak each year. This wood was essential for the bending timbers of small boats such as P.T.'s, mine sweepers, and subchasers.

A million three hundred thousand inductees were processed at Fort Dix, and more than 2,000,000 troops left Camp Kilmer for Europe. The Kilmer location was only open pastureland near Stelton before 1942.

After the war New Jersey turned its attention to its outmoded constitution, and the new constitution of 1947 was accepted. Two years later Governor Alfred E. Driscoll became the first New Jersey governor in more than a century to be elected for a second term, since this was permitted by the new constitution.

More than 160,000 New Jersey men and women were called up during the Korean war, the second largest number of wartime participants in the state's history.

In recent years the coasts of New Jersey have been particularly hard hit by severe hurricanes. The one in 1944 was the heaviest in thirty years. Another of great severity came in 1950, followed by Hazel in 1954, Diane in 1955, and Donna in 1960. Fourteen persons were killed, 1,300 injured, and $100 million worth of property was destroyed in the coastal storm of March, 1962.

The census of 1960 showed that New Jersey, with a population of over six million, had become the second most densely populated state in the nation; later it took first rank.

During 1961 the states of New Jersey, New York, Pennsylvania, and Delaware signed a Delaware River Compact, where all would work together to build dams, recreation projects, and prevent floods.

In 1962 the long-proposed second level of the George Washington Bridge opened. This greatly increased the bridge's capacity.

The state was busy in 1963 with plans to celebrate its 300th birthday, since 1964 would be the tercentenary of the possession of New Jersey by Berkeley and Carteret. This tercentenary has been considered especially important because it was the only statewide celebration ever held in New Jersey. A Tercentenary Commission was at work as early as 1950.

A particularly important part of that celebration was New Jersey's participation in the New York World's Fair of 1964-65. The New Jersey pavilion at the fair featured a section for each of the 21 counties of the state, with the roofs of various sections suspended in midair from slanted posts. The exhibit was approached through a grove of thirty-eight New Jersey willow oaks. Visitors enjoyed a quiet rest in four interior gardens. Outstanding performers and groups from New Jersey were featured throughout the fair period in the central performing arts area. This area was made to resemble four village squares. Bands blared, choirs and choruses raised their voices, folk dancers whirled, and symphony orchestras sounded forth.

In addition to the fair, almost every community in the state participated in the widest possible variety of observances of the tercentennial occasion.

New Jersey closed its first 300 years with a bang, and started hopefully on the next.

During the early years of its fourth century, the state joined the nation in another celebration—the U.S. Bicentennial, in 1976. That year voters approved gambling at Atlantic City casinos, and a state income tax was adopted to finance the public schools.

Also in 1976 the first portion of the $300 million Hackensack Meadowlands development opened with the Giants football and Cosmos soccer teams as the first tenants, and with the race track in operation.

During the 1970s plans were under way for the mammoth industrial center, with containership terminal, on the New Jersey side of Upper New York Bay. Also there were efforts by the state government to lure back the producers of motion pictures, in the hope of regaining New Jersey's former leadership.

Tulip beds and lake in Warinanco Park in Elizabeth.

In another field of entertainment, by the mid-1970s the Miss America Beauty Pageant had become the world's richest scholarship foundation for women, awarding a million dollars annually in grants. Its TV broadcasts have usually attracted the largest audience for any non-sports or non-news telecast.

One way or another, New Jersey appeared likely to continue to attract a large share of national and international attention, adding to its lure of enchantment.

An osprey

Natural Treasures

RESIDING IN THE EARTH

New Jersey has never had large quantities of gold and silver, but it has had other natural riches.

The iron and copper, lead and zinc found so plentifully in early New Jersey were made into more useful objects than could have come from silver or gold. The fertile soil made it the Garden State and helped it feed the soldiers of the American Revolution and, later, helped it supply one of the world's greatest concentration of people.

Many of the mineral riches of New Jersey are unique and unusual, such as the diabase trap rock. Maganiferous residium and greensand marl are produced only in New Jersey. Marl was discovered as early as 1768 and gives its name to Marlboro. It is used for water softeners and fertilizers.

Glass sand, cement rock, slate, clays, and peat moss are important. Franklin has long been known for its world famous zinc deposits. There are no deposits of coal, oil, natural gas, precious metals, or rare earths in New Jersey, but offshore oil reserves are promising.

The sea itself, beating along 127 miles (204 kilometers) of Jersey shore, may soon become one of the richest sources of minerals. Already New Jersey is one of the leading states in separating magnesium from the chemicals in ocean waters.

FIELD, FOREST, AND THE WATERS BENEATH

To some people the fact that New Jersey, although in the midst of the great populations of the East Coast, is still almost half forested would seem completely unbelievable. Yet 46 percent of the state remains under forest cover, though much of this is worthless as timber.

The Pine Barrens cover almost a million and a half acres (607,030 hectares). This is also one of the most thinly populated areas. Twelve state forests protect 150,000 acres (60,700 hectares) of the woodlands of New Jersey. Two hundred varieties of native trees still flourish in the state.

Most of the woodlands to the north are composed of a wide variety of hardwoods. Wherever they are, New Jersey's forests provide timber and pulp, offer recreation to millions of people, and help to conserve the soil and water resources. Whenever the flowering white dogwood burst out in a sea of bloom on the Watchung Hills, people recall how much of the land's beauty is due to its trees.

Fields and forests of New Jersey have an amazing abundance of wildflowers. More than a thousand different kinds of wild beauties are found within the state. New Jersey can boast of fifty varieties of wild orchids that are found in the mysterious Pine Barrens.

About sixty-seven different kinds of birds are native to New Jersey and may be found in the state year round. But 375 species of birds have been seen in New Jersey, including the rare bald eagle and American egret.

A famous refuge for birds, the Witmer Stone Wildlife Sanctuary is maintained by the New Jersey Audubon Society. Visitors thrill as the colonies of herons come home to roost, silhouetted against the setting sun. Terns and black skimmers are common there.

Brigantine Wildlife Refuge is another noted bird sanctuary.

At the Audubon Center of South Jersey at Cape May Court House, ospreys make their nests, and the evening whistle of bob whites is heard regularly.

At Franklin Lakes sanctuary of the Audubon Society, an observation window has been created so that people may see the birds in their natural setting. There are 132 miles (212 kilometers) of New Jersey coastal lands for duck hunters.

Whitetail deer are the largest land animals found in New Jersey. More than 8,000 deer were brought in by hunters during the season of 1962. Thousands of acres in the state are open to hunters in season. Raccoon, squirrels, rabbits, opossum, and muskrat are common. Muskrats are trapped in the Salem County marshes, and their warm furs go to make up many a fashionable coat.

The many waters of New Jersey are home to a surprising variety of

Passaic Falls

fish. Saltwater fishing has become one of the popular sports. Good fishing may be found in albacore, dolphin, tuna, flounder, porgy, and striped bass. Fishing on inland waters offers many a thrill to lovers of angling.

Not all, however, may expect the good fortune that came to Jacob Quackenbush in 1857 when he opened a freshwater mussel near Montclair and found a large pink pearl. The gem was sold to Tiffanys for $1,500 and put in the crown of Empress Eugenie.

THIRSTY LAND, THIRSTY PEOPLE

One natural resource that too many people take for granted is that of fresh water. Great quantities of water are required for manufacture, and growing populations constantly need more. The Delaware Valley Water Authority has an effective long-range conservation program.

Increasing attention is being given to conserving water, creating new reservoirs, and protecting existing supplies from pollution.

New Jersey is fortunate that it has adequate supplies of water for some years ahead. Its rainfall ranks among the heaviest in the country and is quite dependable. Lakes, reservoirs, and underground water are all abundant.

45

The DuPont Company's Chambers Works in Deepwater,
the largest chemical plant in the Western Hemisphere.

The People Use Their Treasures

FROM SOUPS TO NUTS AND BOLTS

New Jersey is one of the great industrial and manufacturing states. It claims to make a greater variety of products than any other state. Ninety percent of all possible types of goods are manufactured in New Jersey. In spite of being one of the five smallest states, it ranks seventh among all the states in the value added to goods by manufacture in its factories.

In the fantastically complicated and important field of chemicals, it is first among all the states. It holds third place in the manufacture of clothing and also is third in producing instruments and clocks, and fifth in electrical machinery.

New Jersey is home to more than sixty of the seventy-five largest manufacturers in the United States.

"EARLY THEY WERE CLEVER"

New Jersey has been a home of manufacturing for almost three hundred years. James Grover established a shop at Shrewsbury to work iron into useful products at the early date of 1674. The thriving Speedwell Ironworks at Morristown supplied munitions to General Washington. The firm is still in business today.

Two of the oldest business organizations in America continue in operation. These are the Proprietors of West New Jersey and the Proprietors of East New Jersey. West was founded in 1677 and East in 1682.

Alexander Hamilton was one of the founders of the Society for Establishing Useful Manufactures, and he chose a site which later became the city of Paterson, America's first planned industrial city.

Strangely, Paterson "became" Washington, D.C. When the society hired city planner L'Enfant to design Paterson, his plan was far ahead of its time, and was not practical for Paterson then. So he used the Paterson plan when he was hired to design Washington.

MADE IN NEW JERSEY

Another of New Jersey's early industries that continues strong even to the present day is the tricky one of glass making. The first glass-making plant in America was set up by Caspar Wister at Salem in 1752.

Glass making grew in importance until the "golden age" of the industry in New Jersey between 1840 and 1860, when a third of all glass made in the United States was produced in the state. Flemington is one of the few remaining centers where fine cut glass is still being produced. The Kimble Glass Company, Division of Owens-Illinois, Vineland, specializes in laboratory glassware, some of great intricacy.

Glass, made with soda ash, is formed into bottles every thirteen seconds by a blast of air at Owens-Illinois, Inc. plant at Bridgeton.

Ceramics have been made in New Jersey since 1685. An important pottery firm was begun at Burlington in 1688 by Dr. Daniel Coxe of London. Walter Lenox created Lenox Ware in 1889, and the company continues to this day to be America's most important porcelain firm. In 1918 President Woodrow Wilson replaced the English china in the White House with a 1,700-piece Lenox set. Other presidents, including Roosevelt and Truman, have replaced the White House china, and always with Lenox. Lenox has built a multi-million dollar plant at Pomona, but keeps its pioneer plant at Trenton.

Paterson took an early lead in a very important field, the manufacture of locomotives.

Machinery pioneer, Isaac M. Singer, built his new sewing machine factory at Elizabethport in 1873. Even at that early date more than 3,000 persons were on his payroll. The company continues today as the best-known name in the sewing machine industry.

A New Jersey manufacturer is one of the leading producers of a kind of device that would not have seemed possible even a few decades ago. Reaction Motors, at Picatinny, produces jet and rocket engines.

FRESH, FROZEN, CANNED, FERMENTED

Because New Jersey has always produced foods and grains, the state has been concerned almost from the beginning with processing methods. Almost from the beginning, the Garden State has been the fresh vegetable market for New York and Philadelphia.

The brewery established by Aert von Putten at Hoboken, in 1642, is generally considered to be the first brewery in the Western Hemisphere. The state continues to be a leader in brewing even today. P. Ballentine and Sons operates the world's largest single brewery plant at Newark, and Newark is often called the "Milwaukee of the East," producing billions of glasses of beer per year.

A New Jersey liquor bottle gave its name to American slang. A glass firm at Glassboro made bottles in the shape of a log cabin. These were filled by a Philadelphia distiller whose name was E.C.

Booz. The bottles came to be called Booz bottles, and the slang term of booze, meaning liquor, grew into common use.

Possibly the best-known names, products of worldwide reputation, belong to some of New Jersey's food processors.

Ever since Joseph Campbell first dreamed of putting soup in tin cans, his name has been associated with leadership in the soup field. The company was founded at Camden in 1869.

Today the aromatic scent of tomatoes and spices has become one of the best-known trademarks of Camden. The Campbell Company works constantly to produce better strains of tomatoes, sells the plants to growers at cost, and contracts to use a grower's entire harvest, taking much of the risk out of a once risky business. During the tomato season the streets leading to the plant are sometimes lined solidly with trucks bulging with millions of plump red tomatoes.

In another field of food processing, Seabrook Farms was one of the pioneers in the production of quick-frozen foods.

FIBERS AND FABRICS

The first factory in America's first industrial city, Paterson, began to produce its printed calico in 1794.

Paterson went on in the textile field to become the leader in one of the most glamorous and heartbreaking business efforts ever carried on in the United States. In the 1830s silk had become so much in demand that everyone in New Jersey seemed to be dreaming of growing mulberry trees to feed to silkworms to produce cocoons to be woven into silk. Some Jersey people went into the venture on a large scale. Ward Cheney Company built a cocoonery serving as a cafeteria for millions of silkworms. Mulberry seedlings became so valuable that thieves often would dig them up in the dead of night and steal hundreds of trees worth perhaps as much as a dollar apiece.

The cold spring of 1839 killed most of the trees and put an end to the silkworm craze, but Paterson continued until 1914 as America's leading city in the production of silk textiles, using imported raw materials.

William and George Clark opened a plant at East Newark in 1865, and employed 2,000 people to do nothing but make thread.

Two of the country's large manufacturers of woolens, Botany and Forstmann, have existed almost side by side in Passaic. Botany was established in 1889 by a German firm. It was this country's first complete textile mill, doing all of its own spinning, weaving, and finishing under one roof. Julius Forstmann, also from Germany, established his firm in 1903.

Two brothers named Johnson from New Brunswick were convinced of the need for prepared antiseptic bandages and other dressings for wounds. It took them many years to persuade medical men of this need, but today their firm of Johnson and Johnson, established at New Brunswick in 1885, is one of the leaders as well as the pioneer in its field.

Benjamin and Edward Annin discovered that marine signal flags were much in demand. Soon their company went into the making of flags exclusively. Today the Annin company is the largest flag maker in the world. Annin flags have draped the casket of Lincoln, and have been the first to fly over the North Pole. They flutter over the parks of the pennant-winning baseball teams. Annin flags are now made in 10,000 different patterns, for most foreign nations and for every use from Boy Scout pennants to weather warning.

New Jersey holds almost a monopoly in the United States in another textile field, the making of Schiffli embroidery. This is done in tiny shops of Weehawken, West New York, Union City, North Bergen, and Guttenberg.

Only two states exceed New Jersey in the production of clothing and all other types of apparel. Passaic is the handkerchief center of the country. There are more individual plants in New Jersey in the apparel industry than in any other field.

A "BOOMING" BUSINESS

New Jersey's biggest single industry, largest employer, and the field in which it outranks all other states in the nation was almost non-existent in the state until 1910. This is the chemical industry. The greatest push to this industry in New Jersey came from World War I. When German dyes, powders, explosives, and other chemicals were cut off by the war, America was forced to make its own in order to survive.

Today, chemicals alone add over two billion dollars per year to New Jersey's wealth. The Deepwater Plant of Du Pont Company at Carney's Point is said to be the largest chemical plant in the Western Hemisphere.

A large proportion of New Jersey chemicals is used to make other products. Some go directly into making consumer goods with well-known trade names. Du Pont, American Cyanamid, Union Carbide, Merck, Hoffman-LaRoche, Ciba, Squibb, Hercules Powder, General Aniline, and Film and Lambert are among the leaders.

Among these names are leading pharmaceutical houses, producing everything from wonder drugs to toothpaste and baby powder.

New Jersey chemical plants turn out enough of certain chemicals to float all the battleships launched in the state. These include sulphuric acid, industrial chemicals, formaldehyde, dyes, and agricultural chemicals.

Such chemicals find their way into a complex variety of products which include synthetic fabrics, explosives, detergents, paints, and plastics.

New Jersey can boast the first plant ever created to make a completely synthetic plastic. This was the plant at Perth Amboy, which turned out a plastic made of phenol and formaldehyde. Today, of course, the number of synthetic plastics can scarcely be counted.

SHAPING EARTH'S TREASURES

Almost as soon as the Lenni Lenape Indians showed the "black stone" to early settlers, New Jersey served as ironmonger of the colonies. The state has pioneered in producing and creating useful products from a variety of minerals. Jersey iron mines were most active in the late 1800s, but some iron is still mined. Basic iron and steel are

52

not now produced in the state to any extent, although a vast amount of steel is used in manufacture there.

Copper mining and working have also been carried on from early times in New Jersey and it continues to be a leading copper smelting and refining state, although most of the ore is brought in. New Jersey has the unbelievable total of one-third of the total copper refining capacity in the country. An interesting sidelight on copper refining is the value of its by-products. One company alone recovered fifty million dollars of gold and silver from its copper ores, almost as an afterthought. Large copper plants operate at Perth Amboy and Carteret.

A vast quantity of petroleum is pumped into the state for refining. The longest pipeline in the United States runs from Longview, Texas, to Bayonne, New Jersey. This is the huge line known affectionately as the "Big Inch." The state ranks among the leading states in petroleum refining and processing, and many of the largest oil firms are located there.

In addition to their use as fuels, petroleum, natural gas, and coal provide an almost limitless variety of chemical products manufactured in New Jersey.

No gold is mined in New Jersey, but Newark has become the leading center of the country in the manufacture of fine gold jewelry. Most of this highly skilled work is done in small and unprepossessing factories, but the city's beautiful gold work is prized around the world. At one time many Newark jewelry makers stamped "made in Paris" on their work because they feared buyers would think Newark jewelry inelegant. No one any longer has this fear.

The leading mineral produced in New Jersey is stone for buildings, roads, ballasts, and other uses. Granite, basalt, gneiss, and diabase are important. Clays, limestone, and sand and gravel are produced in large quantities in New Jersey.

INFINITE VARIETY

One of the most important developments in printing and mass

communication took place at Paterson, where the process for making continuous rolls of printing paper was developed. Hudson, Bergen, and Essex are major paper counties. Wallpaper, rubber, and plastics are all prominent in the New Jersey industrial scene. The state's rubber products include everything from conveyor belts to hot-water bottles. Shipbuilding and automobile assembly are very important.

Among the world's biggest producers of wallboards, insulations, and similar materials is the Johns-Manville plant at Manville. Lumber, wood, and furniture are valued products.

The second largest industrial employer in New Jersey is the electrical goods industry. This vast operation brings almost a billion and a half dollars to the state every year. This is not surprising in view of the pioneering efforts in the state of such electrical wizards as Thomas Edison.

In the Bloomfield and East Orange area is found one of the greatest concentrations of electrical manufacturers in the world.

R.C.A. had its beginnings at Camden. Westinghouse operates eight large plants in the state. Federal Television and Radio employs thousands in its Clifton plant. At Kearny, Western Electric is one of the state's major employers.

The range of electrical equipment includes radios, television parts, motion picture equipment, transmitters, switchboards and telephones, lamps, television sets and cameras, elevators, and many other things.

Many pages would be required to list the products of New Jersey. They would include dolls and electric trains, brooms, steel pens and aircraft carriers, lamp shades and matches.

CENTERS OF INDUSTRY

New Jersey's largest city, Newark, is also its manufacturing center and one of the great industrial cities of the world. It has the greatest variety of manufacturers of any city of comparable size anywhere, and produces more than 300 different types of goods.

The West Orange Laboratory about 1887, called "an invention factory."

Trenton is considered one of the fastest growing business and industrial areas in the country, but it still ranks behind such established centers as Paterson, Jersey City, West New York, and Camden.

One of the giants of industry, Exxon Corporation (formerly Standard Oil of New Jersey), has its headquarters at Flemington, but no huge refineries are located there. The headquarters of this great company at Flemington consists of a sign on a door and a single filing cabinet containing certain papers. The company simply meets certain legal requirements by establishing such a headquarters there because of Hunterdon County's friendly tax rates.

SPOTLIGHT ON THE UNKNOWN

In an age when scientific know-how is king and its importance is growing daily, New Jersey's leadership in scientific research may prove to be its greatest asset in years to come.

Incredibly, about 10 percent of all scientific research laboratories in the United States are in New Jersey. This number is more than 600 laboratories. Even more amazing, these 600 laboratories employ about 18 percent of all research scientists in the country.

These are conservative figures for New Jersey research, because much research is confidential and even classified by the government. It is impossible to measure it completely. Some experts say the figures should be increased by as much as 5 percent.

From colonial times when New Jersey brought in the first engine ever to puff its steam into American air, New Jersey has been a leader in inventiveness.

Thomas Edison established the world's first "brain factory" at Menlo Park. He was the first to realize that many minds highly trained in a variety of fields, working together, could accomplish more than any one person, no matter how brilliant. Edison also realized that New Jersey was a place that offered opportunity for quiet study and yet was in the midst of the great centers of learning and commerce. These are still important considerations for firms that do their research in the state.

Du Pont established the country's first industry-connected laboratory at Pepauno in 1902. In 1937 the first Plexiglass came out of the company's New Jersey research.

Today several of New Jersey's laboratories rank among the mightiest in the world, including those of Exxon and Bell Telephone. Exxon's laboratories are at Linden and Florham Park.

Bell's first laboratory was begun at Whippany in 1926; now Bell also has others at Murray Hill and Holmdel. One of the most far-reaching of Bell's accomplishments was the development of the transistor, which has revolutionized the electronics industry. Already research has shown that the transistor may be replaced by even more fantastic developments. From Bell came Telstar, the world's first communications satellite. Much of Bell's work is highly classified, dealing with the most remote problems of the space age.

Vitamin B_1 was discovered by Robert R. Williams for Hoffman-LaRoche Company. Merck of Rahway developed vitamin B_{12}. Many other vitamin discoveries have been made in the state. The first sulfanilamide was made by American Cyanamid in 1937 at Bound Brook.

The mysteries of plant life, rocket research, cancer, and the improvement of products from dolls to insecticides are only a few targets of New Jersey's continuing research probes.

GARDENERS IN A GARDEN STATE

The state's farmers grow fifty different varieties of vegetables for processing. Thousands of migrant farm workers swarm into New Jersey each year to help at the critical harvest time.

The farmland of New Jersey has the unique distinction of earning more cash per acre than any other state.

Those who think of the orchid as a rare flower should visit the orchid greenhouses of New Jersey. As the leading grower of mainland commercial orchids, the state produces millions of the exotic blooms under glass.

Other New Jersey crops are cranberries and blueberries. New Jersey began to cultivate its wild cranberries in the 1830s; by 1880 the state was growing half of the nation's cranberries. Today New Jersey is third among the states in cranberry production.

One of the few women to become prominent in horticulture was responsible for the interest in blueberries as a table delicacy. Elizabeth White of Whitesbog felt that the wild blueberry could be developed. She asked the "Pineys" (residents of the Pine Barrens) to bring her the largest and best berries they found growing wild and to mark the bushes where they were found. Over the years the best strains were developed and named for the people who found them. In 1916 Miss White marketed the world's first cultivated blueberries. She also worked on improving the native cranberries and holly strains. New Jersey still ranks first in the nation in production of cultivated blueberries.

Because of the tremendous market for trees and shrubs due to the great population centers, the New Jersey area has one of the largest concentrations of nurseries to be found anywhere.

Thomas Edison's Menlo Park laboratory.

Livestock and poultry hold a prominent place in New Jersey agriculture. Surprisingly, to most people, the state ranks fourth in thoroughbred horses.

Milk is the single largest agricultural income producer in New Jersey, and dairy products find a ready market in the metropolitan areas on every side. A pioneer in space-age methods of dairy operation was the Walker-Gordon milk farm at Plainsboro.

Chickens and eggs are big business in New Jersey. Poultry accounts for a full one-third of the state's farm income. Monmouth

County ranks first in the country in number of chickens on farms. Cumberland County is another leading poultry producer.

Turning to other fields, today the state ranks among the top five in tonnage of fish caught. The leading commercial fish is the manhaden. Its oils find their way into the making of such diverse products as lipstick, linoleum, and liquids for the tempering of steel.

KEEP MOVING!

History's main road runs through New Jersey, as someone has said. Because of its strategic location, from the beginning the area was the principal avenue of travel and communications of the eastern American colonies. That situation is not changed even today, for across the 15-mile (24-kilometer) wide "corridor" of New Jersey there flows the greatest concentration of train and motor traffic in the world. Along that diagonal corridor are three-fifths of the people, three-fifths of the factories, most of the laboratories, and all but six of the state's colleges and universities.

The very first improved road in North America, according to some authorities, was hacked through New Jersey by the Dutch. As early as the 1650s Dutch miners were working Jersey copper in the Pahaquarry area. In order to get their ore out they performed the incredible feat of building a road from Pahaquarry to Kingston in New York, a distance of 104 miles (167 kilometers)! That road can still be traveled today.

By 1730 improved roads carried traffic between New York and Philadelphia. Not long afterwards heavy coaches could transport passengers that distance in the "short" space of 30 or 40 hours.

New Jersey's leadership in highways is still unquestioned. The first four-lane highway in the world was constructed between Elizabeth and Newark. The state has the largest percentage of multi-lane highways of any state. The New Jersey Turnpike and Garden State Parkway rank among the principal highways of the world. The Turnpike is possibly the most traveled anywhere. It was built in the record-breaking time of less than two years, opening in 1952. The

Garden State Parkway has earned the reputation as one of the safest highways in the nation. The Pulaski Skyway was the most expensive highway built up to its time.

New Jersey was first to construct traffic circles and the popular cloverleaf intersections for grade separation.

Many important bridges and tunnels give access to the state. The Holland Tunnel was completed in 1927. Ten years later the Lincoln Tunnel opened, the only three-tube vehicular tunnel in the world. For Philadelphia traffic, the Ben Franklin Bridge was opened in 1926, and traffic first crossed Walt Whitman Bridge in 1957.

No other state has such a combination of advantages as afforded New Jersey by the easy access to two great rivers open to ocean navigation, along with two of the greatest port areas of the world, including the ocean trade of Jersey City, Hoboken, and Weehawken, and important wharves on the Delaware as far as Camden.

The shipyards of New Jersey have contributed to ocean traffic since New Jersey timbers first went into wooden ships. Ocean transport entered the nuclear age when the nation's first commercial nuclear ship *Savannah* went down the ways at its Camden shipyard.

Canals have also taken an important place in New Jersey transportation. The Morris Canal, completed in 1831, with an extension to Jersey City in 1836, was called "one of the great engineering feats of its day." It even pulled boats over hills on special inclined planes in places where the hills were too steep to cut through. This canal was the great dream of its originator, George P. MacCulloch.

The Delaware and Raritan Canal was finished in 1834.

But canals could not compete with the railroads. The first charter for a railroad in America was granted in 1815 to Colonel John Stevens, a Hoboken railroad pioneer. He operated the first steam locomotive ever to be run in this country. It chugged over an experimental track of 630 feet (192 meters) near Hoboken in 1825. Commercial railroad service between South Amboy and Bordentown began in 1833. "John Bull," the tiny locomotive that pulled cars over this road, now is at the Smithsonian Institution in Washington.

Today there are more railroad tracks per square mile in New Jersey than in any other state.

Glenmont, the home of Thomas Edison.

New Jersey had a part in the nation's first feat of aviation when Jean Pierre Blanchard made the first balloon ascension, landing in Woodbury after a daring flight from Philadelphia.

Today, the Newark Airport is one of the busiest air terminals of the nation, and Teterboro Airport is also important. Vast new terminal developments are continually under way.

Building of transportation equipment has also been important in New Jersey. Its leadership for many years in locomotive production is well known, but it is somewhat surprising that more than fifty different makes of automobiles have been manufactured in the state. These include such forgotten names as the Red Bug, the Richelieu, Fergus, American Beauty, and Eagle.

The first Ford agency came to New Jersey in an unusual way. Henry Ford lost a race on the beach at Cape May in 1903. In order to get money for railroad fare back to Detroit, Ford had to sell his car to a New Jersey man, and the buyer sold Ford cars from that time on.

*Lock tender's house
on the Delaware
and Raritan Canal.*

COMMUNICATION

Samuel Parker set up the first permanent printing press in New Jersey in 1751. On this press was printed America's first news magazine, the *New American Magazine.* This pioneer periodical discussed current events and history and carried stories and essays.

New Jersey's first newspaper came into being in order to support the Revolution. This was the *Constitutional Gazette,* published in the Burlington print shop of Isaac Collins. The first issue appeared December 5, 1777. Later it was moved to Trenton.

Newspapers with over a hundred thousand circulation in New Jersey today include the Hackensack *Record,* Newark *News,* and Newark *Star Ledger.*

Book publishing in New Jersey is rapidly growing. Many New York publishers are moving their principal operations to New Jersey where costs are far below those of Manhattan. Often only skeleton sales and editorial staffs are left in New York.

But New Jersey is not content with ordinary means of communications. Research by Bell, R.C.A., and other electronic leaders has placed the state in the forefront of space age communications. The amazing Tiros weather satellite and the incredible Telstar satellite both were developed in New Jersey laboratories.

Human Treasures

IN THE PUBLIC EYE

Two presidents of the United States are associated with New Jersey. President Grover Cleveland was born at Caldwell, but his parents took him from the state when he was three.

The other was not a native of New Jersey. However, in New Jersey Woodrow Wilson gained the fame which later made him president.

The Civil War was still strong in most minds when a young minister's son, Tommy Wilson, entered Princeton University. He graduated in 1879, but the university thought so highly of him it called him back in 1890 to be a professor. Twelve years later Thomas Woodrow Wilson became the distinguished president of the great Princeton University.

His theories of history and government became so well known that he was asked to run for governor of New Jersey. It has been said that the politicians of the time felt they could manage this "professor" easily if he became governor and they could keep back the reforms which so many thought were essential.

Wilson promised the people he would end the rule of "bosses" in New Jersey, and was elected by almost 50,000 votes. He set out at once to get fairer election laws and workman's compensation. Along with a corrupt practices act and a strong public utilities commission, these were passed in his first months in office.

Governor Wilson had succeeded with the "New Idea" legislation, first proposed by a young Republican group. Whenever he felt that one of his measures might fail in the state, he would make a thorough tour of New Jersey, explaining his ideas to the voters. He carried this idea with him to the presidency in 1913.

In New Jersey came the climax of the careers of two other prominent figures of American life and American tragedy.

Dawn had scarcely begun that July day in 1804 when two figures stood back to back on the banks of the Hudson at Weehawken. They paced off the required ten paces, turned, and fired. One figure fell.

This was the famous duel in which Aaron Burr killed Alexander Hamilton. Both of them had many associations with New Jersey. In addition to his plan for Paterson, Hamilton had met his bride in the state while he assisted Washington at Morristown during the Revolution.

Aaron Burr was born in Newark. His father had founded Princeton. When Burr and Jefferson were tied in the vote for the presidency of the United States, Hamilton threw his influence toward Jefferson, and Burr was defeated. He had to be content with the post of vice-president.

The bitter Burr never forgot Hamilton's part in taking away from him the highest office in the land. When Hamilton exerted influence to keep Burr from becoming governor of New York and called Burr a man who could not be trusted, the furious Burr demanded a duel.

Cleveland Memorial Tower, the graduate
college of Princeton University, dedicated in 1913.

So it was that New Jersey became the site of one of the most unusual episodes in American history, where the vice-president of the United States murdered the secretary of the treasury. From that moment on, Burr's brilliant career was finished.

Other prominent early public figures included six New Jersey men who signed the Declaration of Independence, John Hart, Abraham Clark, Richard Stockton, John Witherspoon, William Livingston, and Francis Hopkinson. Hopkinson, of Bordentown, also had the honor of designing the Great Seal of the United States.

William Paterson was one of the persons most responsible for the adoption of the "New Jersey Plan" at the United States Constitution Convention. Later, as governor of New Jersey, Paterson supported Hamilton's ideas for an industrial city, and the city was named in his honor.

The first governor of New Jersey as a free state, William Livingston, also served for the longest period of any governor. He was elected for fourteen consecutive terms.

A New Jersey man who later became United States senator from the state also had an extraordinary career. This was Robert Field Stockton, who was born in Princeton in 1796. Among Stockton's unusual assignments was his work in Liberia, where he helped freed slaves from America set up their African republic. He took part in the building of New Jersey canals and railroads. As an engineer he designed the warship *Princeton*. It was the world's first propeller-driven craft.

In 1844 Stockton took 400 important guests down the Potomac on the *Princeton* for a trial run, President Tyler among them. When the huge new naval gun "The Peacemaker" was test fired, it exploded, killing the secretary of state and secretary of the navy. Three others were killed and many, including Stockton, were injured. Fortunately, the president escaped.

IT CAN'T BE DONE! OR CAN IT?

Before he came to Menlo Park, Edison already had invented wax

65

wrapping paper and the stencil duplicator and had improved the telegraph and stock ticker.

From the Edison shop at Menlo Park came the phonograph, electric light, and the forerunner of the radio tube. Altogether Thomas Edison took out three hundred patents during his stay at Menlo Park, and then moved his operations to West Orange in 1882.

For fifty more years the "Wizard of Menlo Park" labored to create more new things of value to mankind. While at West Orange he took out 520 more patents, including improved motion pictures and sound movies, the alkaline storage battery, and magnetic separation of iron ore.

Altogether, 1,093 patents were issued in Edison's name, the greatest number ever to any individual.

The inventor of assembly-line manufacture, Samuel Colt, did most of the developmental work on his Colt revolver in New Jersey but was not successful with it until after he had left the state. His Paterson Patent Arms Company failed in New Jersey.

A New Jersey Episcopal rector would scarcely be expected to turn inventor, but the Rev. Hannibal Goodwin was the first to develop flexible film for photography. He did this work because he was dissatisfied with the fragile glass projected slides and wanted an unbreakable film for his photographic Bible stories.

One of the best-known trademarks came from a New Jersey man, Eldridge R. Johnson, who improved the talking machine. He said it sounded "like a parrot with a sore throat." Johnson was fascinated by a painting he had bought of a small, lovable white dog with his ear cocked to one side at the sound of a phonograph. This was little Nipper, who became known around the world for listening to "His Master's Voice." Johnson developed the first phonograph disk and the first constant speed turntable. He turned the talking machine into a musical instrument. From his work at Camden the RCA organization came into being. The Victor "disc" became the accepted form for records, rather than the Edison cylinder.

An immigrant school teacher from Paterson, John Holland, created the first practical submarine and tested it before wondering crowds in the Passaic River one day in 1878.

Nipper,
"His Master's
Voice."

But New Jersey's least acknowledged transportation leader was John Fitch. This unhappy and unfortunate man, for whom nothing ever seemed to go right, made and operated a successful steamboat on the Delaware, twenty years before Fulton is supposed to have "invented" the steamboat. Almost every delegate to the United States Constitutional Convention in Philadelphia was taken for a ride on John Fitch's steamboat in 1787, but he was ahead of his time and could not make it a success. Defeated and dejected, he committed suicide in 1798.

Infinitely more successful was Samuel F.B. Morse, who developed the telegraph in an old mill at Morristown. He sent the first successful message there in 1838 and revolutionized the world's communication.

BIG BUSINESS

Willis H. Carrier introduced the first mechanical air conditioning into seventy-five homes in northern New Jersey in 1929. His Carrier Engineering Corporation in Newark is still a leader in the field.

Seven years were spent by John L. Mason in perfecting a method of preserving food in sealed glass jars. The "Mason" jar possibly had a more revolutionary effect on improving the standard of living than any single invention up till its time. He started the Consolidated Fruit Jar Co., still at New Brunswick.

In another canned food field, Dr. John T. Dorrance worked out a new method of canning soup. His condensed soups were completely new and became immensely popular. He became sole owner of the Campbell Company and on his death in 1930 his estate was valued at $115,000,000.

Tobacco was the business of James Buchanan Duke, but he invested heavily in the real estate of New Jersey, buying 2,200 acres (890 hectares) along the Raritan. Whenever he thought a natural feature should be changed, he changed it, creating hills, lakes, and forests. This landscaping is thought to have cost in excess of fifteen million dollars.

There are many other leading New Jersey merchants and industrialists. Louis Bamberger gained his fame as a merchant prince in his Newark department store. John Augustus Roebling made wire rope at Trenton and used his rope to build many famous suspension bridges, the most famous being the Brooklyn Bridge. E.R. Squibb and George B. Merck were leaders in the pharmaceutical field. In a somewhat related line, Robert Wood Johnson built his firm of Johnson and Johnson into the largest in the field of bandages and surgical dressings. Another tycoon was John W. Hyatt of Hyatt Roller Bearings. The idea of Charles H. Ingersoll to make inexpensive watches and clocks resulted in his great Ingersoll Watch Company.

MEN OF SCIENCE

Many of the scientific discoveries in New Jersey laboratories have been team efforts. Sometimes, however, an individual like Dr. Selman Waksman of Rutgers University receives great honor. Dr. Waksman was awarded the Nobel Prize for his discovery of streptomycin.

Possibly the most notable scientist in the world's history chose

68

New Jersey as his adopted home. This was the brilliant scientific philosopher-mathematician Albert Einstein. He spent the last years of his life lecturing at the Institute for Advanced Studies at Princeton, where he died in 1955. It was Dr. Einstein, a lover of peace, who was most influential in urging President Franklin D. Roosevelt to start the work that eventually resulted in the atomic bomb.

A nonscientist who was responsible for a "scientific" accomplishment was William F. Allen of South Orange, only one of many who thought something ought to be done about time. In his day there was no standard time. Watches varied. Railroads might use the time of their home office. It was almost impossible to keep an appointment punctually. Then in 1883 Allen worked out a plan to standardize time through the use of various time zones across the country. The nation has operated on Mr. Allen's "standard time" ever since.

PATRIOTS ALL!

New Jersey has given the nation many people famous in history for courage and bravery.

Perhaps the most famous New Jersey hero is Captain James Lawrence of Burlington. During the War of 1812 he was wounded. As he lay dying on his ship, the *Chesapeake,* he spoke one of the most often-repeated phrases ever uttered, "Don't give up the ship."

The commander of America's most famous warship, the *Constitution* (Old Ironsides), was a native of Princeton, Commodore William Bainbridge.

A hero of the war with the Barbary pirates in Tripoli was Captain Richard Somers of Somers Point.

New Jersey produced many heroes of the Revolutionary War. One of the best known of these was a minister. The Rev. James Caldwell was called the "Fighting Parson." He preached on Sunday and fought the other six days. On the pulpit in his church at Springfield he placed two revolvers whenever he preached. In a British attack on Springfield, American troops had only a single cannon. When they began to run out of wadding for the cannon, Rev. Caldwell rushed to the church and came back, arms loaded with Watts hymn books. He had an enormous voice and shouted above the battle, "Here, boys, give 'em Watts. Put Watts into them, boys!" With the aid of the hymnals, the cannon was successful in stopping the British at that spot. Later, the Rev. Caldwell was shot by an American sentry.

FEMININE NEW JERSEY

Many extraordinary and prominent women have called New Jersey home.

One of the best remembered of these is Nurse Clara Maass of East Orange, who volunteered in the Spanish-American War. During that war, in both Cuba and the Philippines, she became aware of the full horror of yellow fever. She volunteered to help with the experiments aimed at finding a cure for yellow fever. The mosquito was thought to be the cause of this disease, but doctors needed proof. Clara Maass courageously volunteered to be bitten, and died in the experiment which helped to rid the world of the scourge of yellow fever. Newark General Hospital, where she graduated, now is called Clara Maass Memorial Hospital in her honor.

Another unusual New Jersey woman was Elizabeth Haddon. In 1701 she came alone to New Jersey from England to undertake what was then a unique assignment for a woman—to manage her father's 500-acre (202-hectare) tract there. In New Jersey she also preached and founded the town of Haddonfield, the only colonial town ever founded by a woman. She continued in her unusual course by proposing marriage to her future husband, John Estaugh. The poet Longfellow tells of their romance in his work "The Theologian's Tale."

Possibly New Jersey's most famous woman is Clara Barton. She became a leading American figure as a nurse in the Civil War. She helped relatives and friends locate almost 40,000 missing Civil War servicemen. In 1880 she became the first American Red Cross president.

Another New Jersey humanitarian was Dorothea Lynde Dix, who

did much to improve conditions in the nation's jails, asylums, and poorhouses.

The names of other famous women of New Jersey include Ann Whitall, Elizabeth White, Tempe Wick, Janetje Tours, Penelope Stout, Dorothy Parker, Cornelia Hancock, Susanna Livingston, and Rachel French.

Clara Maas Memorial stamp.

FRIENDS OF THE MUSES

Even those who do not have much to do with serious poetry are likely to be familiar with one work of a renowned New Jersey poet. In fact, the work is so familiar and well known, it is often parodied and belittled and yet its position in the hearts of all people and its power to move the reader must place it among the really inspired works.

The poet, of course, is Joyce Kilmer and the poem his most famous, the beloved *Trees*. Kilmer was born in New Brunswick, and the great old oak reputed to have inspired the poem was preserved by the College of Agriculture of Rutgers. Joyce Kilmer was killed in World War I at the age of thirty-two, before his talent could grow and mature fully.

A New Jersey poet whose works are not so well known but who was considered by fellow writers to be one of the greatest poets in American history was a product of recent times. This was Dr. William Carlos Williams, a lifelong resident of Rutherford, who left a legacy of forty books of poetry, and yet he considered his main work to be that of a medical man. Dr. Williams died at Rutherford in 1963.

The man who has been called America's greatest poet by many authorities, Walt Whitman, bought a home at Camden in 1873 and lived there for the rest of his life.

Other prominent New Jersey writers include Mary Mapes Dodge, author of *Hans Brinker and the Silver Skates;* Stephen Crane, *The Red Badge of Courage;* Albert Payson Terhune, famous author of dog books and stories and a dog breeder; John Woolman, whose *Journal* is one of the "Harvard Classics"; James Fenimore Cooper, renowned author of frontier and Indian books; and Philip Freneau known as the "Poet of the American Revolution."

Another New Jersey author has the remarkable record of delighting young readers for fifty-two years. Several generations of young people have been enthralled by an animal character created by Howard R. Garis. This was the elegant rabbit gentleman, Uncle Wiggly, whose tall silk hat was never damaged by the thorns in his favorite briar patch. Garis may hold the record for length of service in writing this syndicated column. Together with his wife, Garis also created one of the most popular book series for young people, *The Bobbsey Twins.*

Among prominent artists, New Jersey claims George Inness, who is considered to be the first great American landscape painter. His son, George, Jr., was also a talented New Jersey artist.

Thomas Nast commuted daily by way of the Hoboken ferry from his home in Morristown to create the cartoons that gave him a reputation as possibly the most famous cartoonist who ever lived. He had the unique distinction of creating the Republican elephant and the Democratic donkey and the Santa Claus we know today as a fat jolly man with red suit trimmed in white fur.

Famous New Jersey composers include Lowell Mason, who wrote, among other hymns, the favorite *Nearer, My God, to Thee;* Harry Carrol, whose most famous song perhaps is *I'm Always Chasing Rainbows;* George Anthiel, whose compositions were so modern they caused riots when played in Paris; and the great Jerome Kern of Roselle.

New Jersey can claim the first composer in America. Francis Hopkinson's book *Seven Songs,* published in 1788, is thought to be the first book of music published by any American composer.

SUCH INTERESTING PEOPLE

New Jersey people have so much "bounce," they seem always to be the first off the ground—with the first balloon ride, the first dirigible ride—and on into the space age with a pioneer astronaut. One of America's first men in space was the modern New Jersey hero Walter Schirra, Jr. After his breathtaking six-orbital flight, Commander Schirra returned to his boyhood home, Oradell, for a reception. A marker has been placed there in his honor.

Another New Jersey pioneer, Dr. William Newell, was responsible for creating the nation's first coastal lifesaving stations. In Congress, he introduced the bill which organized the U.S. Lifesaving Service, and the first two lifesaving stations were set up in Ocean County, New Jersey.

In the field of athletics, Arnold Cream took the name of his state when he became "Jersey Joe" Walcott. He later achieved fame as the world's heavyweight boxing champion, beating Ezzard Charles for the title. North New Jersey has been the home of many famous Yankee and Dodger baseball players.

Another New Jersey man who became noted in a field of athletic prowess was Sam Patch, the "Jersey Jumper." Sam had a short but spectacular career in jumping over high falls. He first attracted attention by jumping over the falls of the Passaic and his reputation was worldwide when he succeeded in jumping over Niagara Falls. The *Saturday Evening Post* said his feat was "an act so extraordinary as almost to appear an incredible fable. Sam Patch has immortalized himself." He was killed when he tried to jump over Genesee Falls on a Friday the 13th.

Walter M. Schirra, Jr. was the pilot of the Mercury Atlas 8 flight.

A very large number of show business personalities have called New Jersey home. These include Frank Sinatra, Gordon MacRae, Bud Abbott, Connie Francis, Jerry Lewis, and Ozzie Nelson, to name only a few.

A king came to live in Bordentown in 1816. Joseph Bonaparte had been King of Spain and earlier was King of Naples. When his brother Napoleon was defeated at Waterloo, Joseph fled to America. He bought about 1,800 acres (728 hectares) of land on the beautiful bluffs above the Delaware River and built a mansion where he lived in the style to which a king becomes accustomed.

Joseph Bonaparte was so taken with the values of democratic America he refused to accept the throne of Mexico when it was offered to him, saying, "Every day I pass in this hospitable land proves more clearly to me the excellence of republican institutions for America. Keep them as a precious gift from heaven."

The children of Bordentown loved to skate on Bonaparte's artificial pond during the winter, and the former king enjoyed rolling oranges and apples onto the lake and watching the skaters scramble for them. His neighbors called him the "Good Mr. Bonaparte" to distinguish him from his brother, Napoleon. Joseph Bonaparte lived among them in contentment for eighteen years.

Nassau Hall at Princeton University. New Jersey has two of the oldest universities and colleges in the United States. Princeton University was founded in 1746 and Rutgers, The State University in 1766.

Teaching and Learning

New Jersey was the only colony to have two colleges before the Revolutionary War, and these two—Princeton and Rutgers—are still among the best known in the nation.

Princeton was founded at Elizabeth in 1746 and called at that time the College of New Jersey. It moved to Princeton in 1756 and occupied Nassau Hall, which was then the largest stone building in the Colonies. Its name was not changed to Princeton until 1896, on the 150th anniversary of its founding. The Rev. Jonathan Dickinson was the first president of Princeton, which began as a Presbyterian institution. Aaron Burr's father was the second president.

Another of Princeton's presidents was Andrew McCosh. It is a strange coincidence that Dr. McCosh's theory of the universe was widely accepted before another great scientist-philosopher, Albert Einstein, wrote his theory of the universe. Later Einstein also came to Princeton to take a leading part in the Institute for Advanced Studies there. This institute is the only one of its kind. It has been called a kind of "intellectual hotel" where leading figures in science, literature, and the arts are given an opportunity to produce their works, study, or teach under the best possible conditions.

It is interesting to note that President Woodrow Wilson was the first president of Princeton who was not a clergyman. In his honor a division of the university is called the Woodrow Wilson School of Public and International Affairs.

At Princeton's James Forrestal Research Center the principal effort is aimed at developing a source of universal energy through concentrated research at the Plasma Physics Laboratory.

Rutgers is the only college of Colonial times to evolve into both a land-grant college and a state university. It was founded by Dutch settlers in New Brunswick in 1766 and was called Queen's College, and is the nation's eighth oldest institution of higher learning. It became the state university of New Jersey in 1945. It has a branch of medicine and dentistry at Newark.

Other four-year colleges in New Jersey are state operated. Prominent private institutions in the state include Seton Hall University,

The University Chapel at Princeton University.

South Orange; Fairleigh Dickinson University, Rutherford; and Drew University, Madison.

New Jersey Institute of Technology is a leading technical school. Stevens Institute of Technology at Hoboken has among its many resources the Davidson Laboratory. This is the largest privately operated hydrodynamic laboratory in the world. Designs of many famous and important ships have been tested there. Princeton Theological Seminary is one of the best known in ministerial and church education. Another New Jersey college that instructs in a unique church field is the Westminster Choir College at Princeton.

The first school in New Jersey was founded at Bergen in the early 1660s. More than two hundred years later, in 1871, New Jersey's public school system was made entirely free. Since that time it has come to be known as one of the best in the nation. New Jersey pioneered in the fields of teacher tenure and retirement. The first high school in New Jersey was begun at Newark and is among the oldest in the United States. Lawrenceville is one of the great private schools of the nation.

Enchantment of New Jersey

THE NORTHEAST CORNER

George Washington Bridge has been called the "Gateway to New Jersey." The visitor who approaches by way of this "gate" will be struck first by the same mighty palisades that greeted Henry Hudson, the first visitor. They stretch far away in both directions.

Coming across the bridge the visitor can see the site of old Fort Lee, which failed to protect Washington and his men from the British assault. He might even still be able to spot the very rocks to which Pearl White clung in her movie adventures.

Not far to the north is the area of Palisades Interstate Park.

Coming south again, the Garden State Parkway, one of the finest highways in New Jersey, brings the visitor close to almost every attraction of the state's eastern shores.

Historic Paterson, America's first planned industrial city, is nearby, with its memories of Alexander Hamilton. It is not far from the Hudson bluff where he met his violent death. Paterson has particular meaning to Sunday school teachers and pupils, for one of the first Sunday schools was established there in 1794. The historic falls of the Passaic are visible now only in times of very high water. The world's first submarine may be seen at the Paterson Museum.

To the east of the parkway are Newark and Jersey City, the first and second cities of the state in population.

Among the many attractions of Jersey City is the Colgate Clock. Its mammoth minute hand weighs more than a ton (.9 metric ton) and races 23 inches (58 centimeters) each minute in order to complete its huge circle in an hour.

Fortunate is the visitor who reaches Newark in mid-April, for this industrial city offers one of the world's finest and possibly least known blossom displays. More than five thousand oriental cherry trees have been propagated and carefully cultivated in Branch Brook Park. This is a more brilliant display than is offered by the cherry trees at Washington. A wide variety of types and colors of blossoms has been cultivated. Several of these are double, while the famous blossoms around the Tidal Basin in Washington are single. The Newark blossoms have been called the greatest display of such blooms in the United States.

Newark has a large and fine museum and planetarium. The museum offers one of the finest displays in the country on Tibet. Another Newark showplace is the Catholic Cathedral of the Sacred Heart. The sculpture "Wars of America" by the prominent sculptor Gutzon Borglum is another Newark attraction.

It is strange to think of a great city as a leading "forester," but Newark controls its watershed in order to assure a steady supply of good water. The city is one of the leaders in developing and practicing forest conservation.

In nearby North Bergen the annual Plattdeutsches Volkfest is a colorful American folk festival.

To the west of the parkway the traveler may see the birthplace of Grover Cleveland at Caldwell.

Somewhat farther south, to the west of the parkway, is the Thomas Edison country. The federal government has created a National Monument and Museum to preserve the great inventor's home and workshop at West Orange, where he labored for forty-four years. The many Edison inventions displayed there are the authentic originals, including the very first phonograph. His disordered desk is just as he left it. On the grounds is the motion picture studio where much of the first full-length movie, "The Great Train Robbery," was made

At Menlo Park, where the inventor first established himself in New Jersey, a great memorial shaft has been erected, topped by an enormous light bulb 14 feet (4 meters) tall. The first electric railroad locomotive also may be seen here.

THEY SELL SUNSHINE BY THE SEASHORE

After the parkway crosses the turnpike, the visitor is never far from the 127-mile (204-kilometer) stretch of New Jersey seashore which has been called the Riviera of America. There are more than

Wars of America Memorial in Newark.

sixty resort towns along the Atlantic. This stretch of shore has contributed a whole new chapter to American "culture"—the picture postcard, saltwater taffy, boardwalks, the entertainment pier, and particularly bathing beauty contests.

Closest to the metropolitan areas, with a fine view of the New York harbor, is Atlantic Highlands. Nearby, the long finger of Sandy Hook points to where Verrazano first found the entrance to the great harbor of New York. The old lighthouse on Sandy Hook is the oldest continuously established navigation light in the country. Ever since the days of the Dutch there has been a light there to guide the vessels to New York. Sandy Hook is now protected as a state park.

Where Sandy Hook hooks on to the mainland is Long Branch. This was one of the most popular early resorts. General Grant was given a summer home there in 1868, donated by his admirers. The resort became a second home to such well-known personalities as Diamond Jim Brady, Lillie Langtry, and Jim Fisk. Gamblers and other shady characters found a haven there and it was usually considered a rather wicked place by its neighbors. However, its questionable characteristics soon began to fade.

Long Branch's neighbor, Ocean Grove, was started as a religious resort in 1869. It grew rapidly, and the camp meeting services were attended by as many as 6,000 people.

Today, Ocean Grove is still one of the most unusual resorts anywhere. It is labeled "God's square mile of health and happiness."

The nearby community of Asbury Park was founded in 1871 and named in honor of the first Methodist bishop in the United States, Francis Asbury. Today Asbury Park annually celebrates the arrival of Columbus and is the site of the International Miniature Golf Tournament. It occupies somewhat the same position on the north coast of the state as Atlantic City does on the south, as a popular convention spot.

One of New Jersey's newest state parks has been created on the long, incredibly thin stretch of Atlantic shore called Island Beach. This is one of the few unspoiled beach areas remaining along the Atlantic Coast. Its rare dunes, birds, trees, and plants are given permanent protection for the enjoyment of all. Here, too, is famed "Old Barney," historic Barnegat Lighthouse.

To the west are the mysterious Pine Barrens, surrounded by civilization and yet one of our few remaining true primitive wilderness areas. Here orchids and a wide variety of wild flowers can be seen in great profusion.

Another attraction of the area is the state-owned Wharton Tract of 95,000 acres (38,445 hectares). Included in the tract is the restored glass making and iron making village of Batsto.

Each year millions of visitors flock to Atlantic City. This once sleepy "bathing village" now has the world's most famous boardwalk, 60 feet (18 meters) wide and 5 miles (8 kilometers) long. As many as 300,000 people enjoy the boardwalk in a single day. The

*Ocean Grove
Auditorium.*

popular rolling chairs were first used in 1884. The largest hall in the world, seating 41,000, also containing the largest organ, helps the city to maintain its convention leadership. The latest attraction is gambling, now legal in Atlantic City.

Nearby Margate is famous, among other things, for Lucy. Lucy is an elephant, but a very unusual one, with legs 10 feet (3 meters) across and 20 feet (6 meters) high and a 36-foot (11-meter) trunk. In 1882 a Margate promoter spent almost $40 thousand to build Lucy to help advertise the attractions of the area, and she has been a Margate landmark ever since.

In the vicinity of Atlantic City is one of the truly authentic "ghost towns" of the East. In 1822 James Allaire created a model village to house the five hundred laborers in his metal-working establishment. When the works were closed Allaire became a deserted village. Today the area is maintained as a state park with houses, stores, and iron works much as they were in their boom days.

At Pomona is the National Aviation Facilities Experimental Station.

The most famous New Jersey sea resort in early times was Cape May. Before the Civil War this was the country's most popular and best-known resort, host to presidents and other prominent people. Visitors may often be seen roaming its famous beaches with bowed heads as if in meditation. They are probably searching for the famous "Cape May Diamonds," which are pieces of pure quartz, polished and smoothed by the waves and much sought as souvenirs, although they have no commercial value.

A SOUTHERN CLIME

Many locations in southern New Jersey hold the visitor's attention. Millville is noted as the "Holly City of America." The oyster fleet at Port Norris and the monument to the Greenwich Tea Party are attractions of the southwest section. At Salem is the famous old Salem Oak and the Delaware Memorial Bridge. Visitors to nearby Finn's Point National Cemetery remember the suffering of Confederate soldiers at the location where almost 2,500 of them have their last resting place.

The southern New Jersey city of Vineland was a planned community with a difference. Its founder, Charles K. Landis, was convinced that a community could be created where people with very moderate means could become successful. He helped his settlers with loans and good advice. He worked hard, and before he died in 1900 almost everything he hoped for had come true in Vineland. At Vineland today, also, is one of the world's leading schools for training the retarded.

BY THE MIGHTY RIVER

Camden offers 14 miles (23 kilometers) of port frontage for the world's trade. Everything from pen points to battleships is made in its factories. The drafting room of the New York Shipbuilding Corporation there has a half acre (.2 hectares) of drafting table surfaces. The city, of course, has close ties with Philadelphia just across the river. A major attraction for visitors there is the house and tomb of the leading American poet Walt Whitman.

The Camden suburb of Haddonfield is the site of Indian King Tavern where the legislature met in 1777 to declare that New Jersey was now an independent state. Also at Haddonfield occurred the first major discovery of dinosaur bones in the United States. On the farm of John E. Hopkins in 1858 was uncovered the remains of a hadrosaurus, a monster that towered to a height of 30 feet (9 meters). Before he realized their scientific value Mr. Hopkins had given away many of the bones as souvenirs.

At Burlington, two homes have been preserved—those of Naval hero James Lawrence, and noted writer James Fenimore Cooper.

Founded by Mahlon Stacy in 1679, a settlement called "The Falls" soon came to be known as Trent's Town, then became Trenton in honor of early landholder Colonel William Trent. One of the attractions of Trenton today is the well-preserved home of the man who gave the city his name.

The capitol dome in Trenton.

Almost as soon as the city became the state capital in 1790, plans were laid to create a suitable capitol building. One of the state's greatest bargains was the price of the land where the capitol was to be built—five shillings. In 1794 the original capitol was finished. New Jersey is one of the few states in which the original state capitol building is still included as a portion of the present-day capitol structure. The rotunda and porticoes were added in 1848 and the grounds landscaped. In 1889 damage from a fire of 1885 was repaired and the present front section added. The Assembly Chamber and Senate Chamber also were built later, to bring the building to its present form. The corridors of the capitol are lined with historical portraits.

Although its capitol building is old, the capital city has one of the newest and finest of cultural centers, completed in honor of the tercentennial celebration of 1964. On a site of 10 acres (4 hectares) overlooking the Delaware, the state has created a complex including the state library, a planetarium, auditorium, and the fine state museum.

Garden State Arts Center is a noteworthy home of ballet and other cultural activities.

Near the heart of Trenton is a fine granite shaft. This marks the spot where General Washington placed his cannon in Trenton's most noted historic event, the first Battle of Trenton during the Revolution. Still preserved for visitors are the old barracks of pre-Revolutionary time. This is generally considered to be the best existing example of Colonial barracks in the United States.

North and west of Trenton is Washington Crossing State Park, site of McKonkey Ferry House, where the general made his famed and daring crossing of the Delaware in preparation for the Battle of Trenton.

Nearby is Lambertville where the Music Circus presented the first tent-in-the-round musical show ever given.

NEW JERSEY'S "MIDDLE"

Official home of the governor of New Jersey is Morven, which is not in Trenton, but in Princeton. This historic house was donated to the people of the state by former Governor Walter E. Edge and was first officially occupied in 1957.

A principal attraction of Princeton is Nassau Hall, the first building of the university. This has been called one of the most notable and historic buildings of America, and is now a National Monument.

At Princeton cemetery are the graves of many of the university's presidents.

Two of the most interesting university buildings are the Geological Museum and the Museum of Historic Art.

Princeton Battlefield State Park commemorates the site where Washington again was victorious against the British.

At nearby Rockingham are preserved other memories of the general, who was staying there when he delivered his famous farewell address to the armies.

New Brunswick is noted, of course, as the central home of New Jersey's second pre-Revolutionary university, the State University, Rutgers.

North central New Jersey is one of America's most historic areas. Here in 1933 the United States government created the country's first National Historical Park. Here may be found the home of the widow Ford, where Washington had his headquarters during the worst winter in a hundred years, and a fine historical museum and library. Another reminder of that awful winter is old Fort Nonsense, built by Washington to keep his troops occupied.

In the early 1900s Morristown had another distinction. More than ninety millionaires are said to have lived within 3 miles (5 kilometers) of the village green, a greater concentration than was to be found anywhere else at that time.

Today Morristown is the home of the Seeing Eye headquarters. Mrs. Dorothy Harrison Eustis founded this unique institution which trains dogs to lead the blind.

Another feature of Morris County is the great swamp that has become a National Wildlife Refuge.

NORTHEAST BEAUTIES

Beautiful Lake Hopatcong is one of the great pleasure resources of the state.

Another scenic spot favored by visitors is the Delaware Water Gap, where the views are superb.

In the far north, Sussex County has much justification for claiming to be the most scenic area of the state. High point of the scenery here is called just that, "High Point" State Park, where the states of New York, Pennsylvania, and New Jersey meet in beauty amid lakes and mountains. On clear days the Delaware Water Gap may be seen, more than 80 miles (129 kilometers) away. The highest point in New Jersey is marked by a fine War Memorial Monument, a shaft reaching 225 feet (69 meters) into the air.

FROM MANY NATIONALITIES, ONE PEOPLE

Among the most interesting places in the state are those founded and developed by people of a particular nationality or religious faith.

More than one book could be written about the contributions of

The Society of Friends (Quaker) meeting house in Stoney Brook, erected in 1760.

the Quakers alone. Quakers John Fenwick and William Penn were important in the early settlement of New Jersey. Salem, Burlington, and other Quaker settlements were home to more than 1,400 Quakers in the early 1680s.

Swedes, Dutch, Scots, Irish, and Swiss all have left their marks of improvement on the state—railroads, canals, embroidery factories, towns, and villages.

Egg Harbor City was founded as a German community. Its city council conducted business in German, and typical German activities were organized. It kept its German qualities until well into the twentieth century.

During World War II, displaced persons from Estonia and Japanese-Americans from the West Coast came to work at Seabrook Farms, and after the Red Chinese took over Mongolia, New Jersey welcomed the coming of the little-known Kalmuks to the region around Farmingdale. These followers of the Dalai Lama set up a handsome temple in a cinder-block garage. They did well, and accepted American customs quickly, but they try to maintain many of the gracious and interesting customs and traditions.

A large number of Puerto Ricans are also finding homes in New Jersey today.

So it is throughout the state: New Jerseyans take pride in their state and help to improve it, whether their ancestors came with the Dutch in the 1600s or with the latest group of immigrants.

Handy Reference Section

Instant Facts

Became the third state, December 19, 1787
Capital—Trenton, founded 1679
Nickname—The Garden State
State motto—Liberty and Prosperity
State bird—Eastern goldfinch
State tree—Red oak
State flower—Purple violet
State song—"New Jersey Loyalty" (unofficially)
Area—8,219 square miles (21,287 square kilometers)
Rank in area—46th
Coastline—127 miles (204 kilometers)
Shoreline—1,792 miles (2,884 kilometers)
Greatest length (north to south)—166 miles (267 kilometers)
Greatest width (east to west)—57 miles (92 kilometers)
Geographic center—Mercer
Highest point—1,803 feet (550 meters), High Point State Park, Sussex County
Lowest point—Sea level
Number of counties—21
Population—8,300,000 (1980 projection)
Rank in population—8th
Population density—915 persons per square miles (353 persons per square kilometer) 1970 census
Rank in density—First
Population center—In Middlesex County, 2.8 miles (4.5 kilometers) east of New Brunswick
Birthrate—13 per 1,000 people
Infant mortality rate—15.6 per 1,000
Physicians per 100,000—156

Principal cities—		
Newark	381,930	(1970 census)
Jersey City	260,350	
Paterson	144,824	
Elizabeth	112,654	
Trenton	104,786	
Camden	102,551	

You Have a Date with History

1498—John Cabot sighted territory now called New Jersey
1524—Giovanni de Verrazano passed New Jersey coast
1609—Henry Hudson, first European to touch New Jersey shore
1638—New Sweden founded on Delaware River
1660—Bergen (Dutch) became first permanent New Jersey settlement
1664—English gain control and area called New Jersey
1676—New Jersey divided into East and West territories
1738—Lewis Morris first governor of a united New Jersey
1746—College of New Jersey (Princeton) chartered
1753—First steam engine in America pumped flooded mine at Arlington
1758—America's first Indian reservation, at Brotherton
1766—Queens College (Rutgers) founded
1776—New Jersey Provincial Congress declared independence
1779—Washington and troops at Morristown
1787—New Jersey becomes third state to ratify Constitution
1790—Trenton chosen state capital
1804—Hamilton-Burr duel
1831—First railroad partially operated
1844—New state constitution
1854—Atlantic City founded
1861—New Jersey Volunteers reached Washington
1877—First phonograph operated at Menlo Park
1884—Grover Cleveland elected, only native New Jersey president
1912—Woodrow Wilson elected president
1931—George Washington Bridge opened
1937—Dirigible *Hindenburg* destroyed at Lakehurst
1948—Transistor perfected
1962—Telstar, made in New Jersey, orbited
1964—Statewide Tercentennial celebration
1969—Hackensack Meadowlands Development Commission set up
1972—New Jersey Sports Complex begun
1976—Voters approve gambling in Atlantic City casinos; State income tax adopted

Thinkers, Doers, Fighters

People of Renown Who Have Been Associated with New Jersey

Bonaparte, Joseph
Boudinot, Elias
Boyden, Seth

Kearny, Philip
Kearny, Stephen Watt
Kilmer, Joyce

90

Burr, Aaron
Campbell, Joseph
Cooper, James Fenimore
Crosby, Harrison W.
Dix, Dorothea Lynde
Dodge, Mary Mapes
Dorrance, John T.
Edison, Thomas Alva
Einstein, Albert
Fitch, John
Hancock, Cornelia
Holland, John
Hopkinson, Francis
Johnson, Robert Wood

Lawrence, James
Lenox, Walter
Ludwig, Mary Hays (Molly Pitcher)
Maass, Clara
Mason, John L.
Price, Rodman M.
Singer, Isaac M.
Stevens, John
Stockton, Robert F.
Waksman, Selman
White, Elizabeth
Williams, Robert R.
Williams, William Carlos
Wilson, Thomas Woodrow

Governors of New Jersey

William Livingston 1776-1790
William Paterson 1790-1792
Richard Howell 1792-1801
Joseph Bloomfield 1801-1812
Aaron Ogden 1812-1813
William S. Pennington 1813-1815
Mahlon Dickerson 1815-1817
Isaac H. Williamson 1817-1829
Peter D. Vroom 1829-1832
Samuel L. Southard 1832-1833
Elias P. Seeley 1833
Peter D. Vroom 1833-1836
Philemon Dickerson 1836-1837
William Pennington 1837-1843
Daniel Haines 1843-1844
Charles C. Stratton 1845-1848
Daniel Haines 1848-1851
George F. Fort 1851-1854
Rodman M. Price 1854-1857
William A. Newell 1857-1860
Charles S. Olden 1860-1863
Joel Parker 1863-1866
Marcus L. Ward 1866-1869
Theodore F. Randolph 1869-1872
Joel Parker 1872-1875
Joseph D. Bedle 1875-1878
George B. McClellan 1878-1881

George C. Ludlow 1881-1884
Leon Abbett 1884-1887
Robert S. Green 1887-1890
Leon Abbett 1890-1893
George T. Werts 1893-1896
John W. Griggs 1896-1898
Foster M. Voorhees 1899-1902
Franklin Murphy 1902-1905
Edward C. Stokes 1905-1908
John Franklin Fort 1908-1911
Woodrow Wilson 1911-1913
James F. Fiedler 1914-1917
Walter E. Edge 1917-1919
Edward I. Edwards 1920-1923
George S. Silzer 1923-1926
A. Harry Moore 1926-1929
Morgan F. Larson 1929-1932
A. Harry Moore 1932-1935
Harold G. Hoffman 1935-1938
A. Harry Moore 1938-1941
Charles Edison 1941-1944
Walter E. Edge 1944-1947
Alfred E. Driscoll 1947-1954
Robert B. Meyner 1954-1962
Richard J. Hughes 1962-1970
William T. Cahill 1970-1974
Brendan T. Byrne 1974-

Index

page numbers in bold type
indicate illustrations

92

94

PICTURE CREDITS

ABOUT THE AUTHOR

With the publication of his first book for school use when he was twenty, **Allan Carpenter** began a career as an author that has spanned more than 135 books. After teaching in the public schools of Des Moines, Mr. Carpenter began his career as an educational publisher at the age of twenty-one when he founded the magazine *Teachers Digest.* In the field of educational periodicals, he was responsible for many innovations. During his many years in publishing, he has perfected a highly organized approach to handling large volumes of factual material: after extensive traveling and having collected all possible materials, he systematically reviews and organizes everything. From his apartment high in Chicago's John Hancock Building, Allan recalls, "My collection and assimilation of materials on the states and countries began before the publication of my first book." Allan is the founder of Carpenter Publishing House and of Infordata International, Inc., publishers of *Issues in Education* and *Index to U. S. Government Periodicals.* When he is not writing or traveling, his principal avocation is music. He has been the principal bassist of many symphonies, and he managed the country's leading non-professional symphony for twenty-five years.